PENGUIN BOOKS

England and the Aeroplane

David Edgerton will from mid-2013 be Hans Rausing Professor of the History of Science and Technology and Professor of Modern British History at King's College London. He is the author of a sequence of groundbreaking books on twentieth-century Britain: *Science, Technology and the British Industrial 'Decline', 1870–1970*; *Warfare State: Britain, 1920–1970*; and *Britain's War Machine*, published by Penguin. He is also the author of the iconoclastic and brilliant *The Shock of the Old: Technology and Global History Since 1900*.

England and the Aeroplane

Militarism, Modernity and Machines

DAVID EDGERTON

PENGUIN BOOKS

PENGUIN BOOKS

Published by the Penguin Group
Penguin Books Ltd, 80 Strand, London WC2R ORL, England
Penguin Group (USA) Inc., 375 Hudson Street, New York, New York 10014, USA
Penguin Group (Canada), 90 Eglinton Avenue East, Suite 700, Toronto, Ontario, Canada M4P 2Y3
(a division of Pearson Penguin Canada Inc.)
Penguin Ireland, 25 St Stephen's Green, Dublin 2, Ireland (a division of Penguin Books Ltd)
Penguin Group (Australia), 707 Collins Street, Melbourne, Victoria 3008, Australia
(a division of Pearson Australia Group Pty Ltd)
Penguin Books India Pvt Ltd, 11 Community Centre, Panchsheel Park, New Delhi – 110 017, India
Penguin Group (NZ), 67 Apollo Drive, Rosedale, Auckland 0632, New Zealand
(a division of Pearson New Zealand Ltd)
Penguin Books (South Africa) (Pty) Ltd, Block D, Rosebank Office Park,
181 Jan Smuts Avenue, Parktown North, Gauteng 2193, South Africa

Penguin Books Ltd, Registered Offices: 80 Strand, London WC2R ORL, England

www.penguin.com

First published as *England and the Aeroplane: An Essay on a Militant and Technological Nation* by Macmillan Press, in association with the Centre for the History of Science, Technology and Medicine at the University of Manchester 1991
This revised edition published in Penguin Books 2013
001

Set in 12.5/14.75pt Garamond MT Std
Typeset by Jouve (UK), Milton Keynes
Printed in England by Clays Ltd, St Ives plc

ISBN: 978-0-141-97516-0

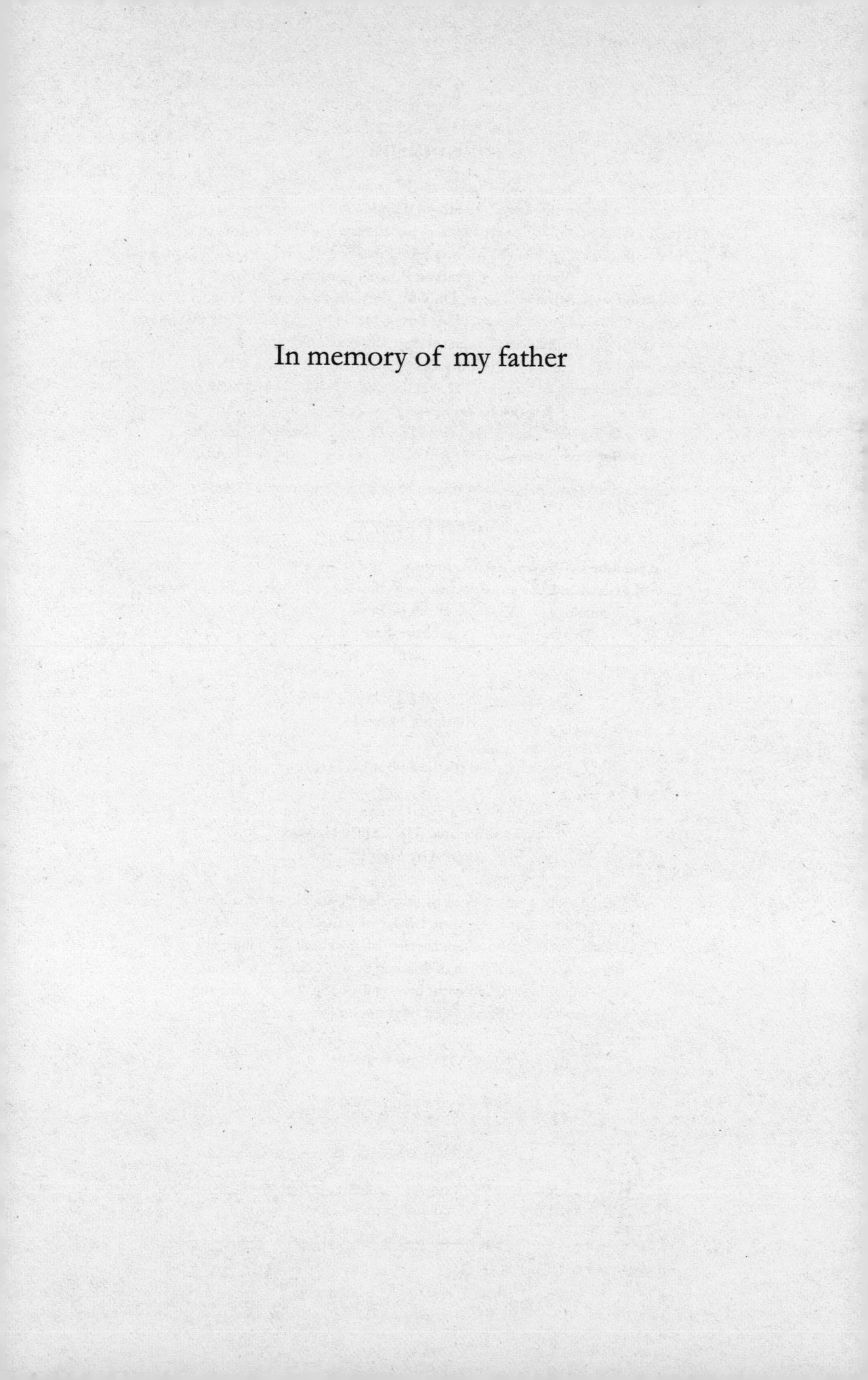

In memory of my father

Contents

List of Diagrams

List of Illustrations

List of Abbreviations

ACA	Advisory Committee on Aeronautics
BAC	British Aircraft Corporation
BALPA	British Airline Pilots' Association
BSE	Bristol Siddeley Engines
CID	Committee of Imperial Defence
CND	Campaign for Nuclear Disarmament
DSIR	Department of Scientific and Industrial Research
MAP	Ministry of Aircraft Production
Mintech	Ministry of Technology
NGTE	National Gas Turbine Establishment
NPL	National Physical Laboratory
RAE	Royal Aircraft Establishment
RAF	Royal Air Force
R&D	Research and Development
RFC	Royal Flying Corps
RNAS	Royal Naval Air Service
SBAC	Society of British Aircraft Constructors

Preface to the New Edition

When it was first published *England and the Aeroplane* was out of kilter with what was known and what was believed about its twin subjects, more so than was readily apparent. It told a series of stories about machines, modernities and militarism which did not fit within then standard British political, ideological, cultural and economic history, let alone histories of aviation. British machines, militarism and modernity were thought to be deeply backward, and British militarism was supposed by some not even to exist. While the book still has, I trust, the power to surprise, it has lost the power to shock, and that, I flatter myself, is to some small extent a measure of its success. But the key point is that twentieth-century British history is now understood in very different ways than it was twenty years ago.

The book essentially told a new story of British aviation, explaining it with a fresh account of key aspects of British history. Yet it was telling that much of the reaction to the book when it was first published in 1991 was concerned with the British 'decline' – the issue of the moment and for long after. *England and the Aeroplane* was indeed radically at odds with what it labelled 'declinist' histories of Britain, a term I coined I think. Declinism dominated not just economic history, but military, political and cultural history to an extent now difficult to recapture. Declinist accounts had enormous authority and moral power, on the left and on the right. They sought to explain what had gone wrong with Britain, and thus what to do to make Britain great again. In these stories, aeroplanes played their part. For some, the failure to support aviation was a cause of decline, or evidence of lack of commitment to modernity, though for others support for particular kinds of aeroplanes pointed to misdirected effort, mainly in support of Empire and the military. Thus though most readers took the book to be an attack on declinism, some also thought I had strengthened the argument that imperialism and militarism were causes of decline.

The essential problem of declinism was that it sought to explain Britain's undoubted relative decline in terms of British failure, when most was the work of foreigners catching up with Britain. It ended up inverting historical reality, making Britain weak in the past, when it was in fact relatively stronger, and weaker than countries it was stronger than. Both what was being described and how it was being explained was, bluntly, far removed from historical reality. Reading these declinist histories, of things that never happened with explanations that can't work, one is tempted to think that anything goes. Yet only a small number of types of failures and explanations and foreign examples dominated – there was a profound and revealing consensus on certain key points and comparisons, from left to right. I came to see what I called a militarist and technocratic critique (both profoundly nationalist), as being central to a wide range of declinist analyses, and histories of Britain more generally. This was revealed in the extraordinary extent to which a place which looked a bit like the pre-1914 German Empire figured in accounts of the British decline, a country which British analysts held organized its armed forces properly and gave due deference to science and engineering. I developed these insights in two articles I published the same year as *England and the Aeroplane.* They addressed the work of two influential declinists from the right and left, Correlli Barnett and Perry Anderson ('The Prophet Militant and Industrial: The Peculiarities of Correlli Barnett', *Twentieth Century British History*, 2 (1991), pp. 360–79; 'Liberal Militarism and the British State', *New Left Review*, 135 (1991), pp. 138–69). The first essay dissected a particularly important form of declinism, while the second extended the fresh account of British militarism which is central to *England and the Aeroplane* by looking also at British naval power and nuclear weapons. Together they set out not only a critique of declinism, but more importantly a new account of the British state and through that of twentieth-century British history which I took forward in subsequent works.

The work of Barnett and Anderson, and Martin Wiener, and the advocates of a 'gentlemanly capitalism' thesis, was being challenged at around the same time as this book first appeared. What was being criticized was generally a particular explanation of decline; there was usually a sense that a better explanation was available or needed. *England and the Aeroplane* saw the key problem not simply as wrong-headed explanations for a well-established phenomenon but rather sought to change what needed to be explained as well as how it was explained. Labelling and rejecting declinism meant casting aside not simply the issue of decline but the assumptions built into declinist histories, which as it turned out had lives of their own. The point of this book was not to engage in a debate on decline or its supposed causes, but to break out of the whole problematic in order to get at British history and the history of British machines in a fresh way. Looking at the history of the aeroplane anew did indeed open up a narrative with unfamiliar ideologies, enthusiasms and ideas.

England and the Aeroplane was written during the commemorations of the fiftieth anniversary of the start of the Second World War; it was finished as the fiftieth anniversaries of the Battle of Britain and the Blitz were about to be marked. The aeroplane, British and German, was and remains central to the British national myths of wartime, in a way warships or merchant ships, let alone tanks and artillery do not. In its treatment of the war this book sought not so much to rethink the Battle of Britain and the Blitz and its myths but rather to put the historiography of Britain at war on a new basis, one in which the aerial defence of Britain and the Blitz and its supposed effects (above all the creation of a welfare state) were not the main and sometimes only stories. For me much more important was the fact that Britain was committed, long before the war, to a strategy of strategic bombing, and that it launched bombers on Germany, unsuccessfully, in May 1940, before the Blitz of late 1940 and early 1941, even before the Battle of Britain of the summer of 1940. By contrast, Angus Calder's *The Myth of the Blitz* (which appeared just after *England and the Aeroplane*), an important reconsideration of wartime history from within a national social democratic perspective, still focussed on the Blitz and the welfare state, though now challenging received wisdom about both.

Putting the British bomber, rather than the British fighter and the German bomber, in the centre of the picture is no easy task both because the Blitz was so central to the overall history of Britain at war, and because the story of British aviation during the war as a whole is so strongly associated with fighters. The association of terror bombing with the Nazis, to which the British were to respond on a greater scale, was and is deep seated. After the war, especially on the left and among liberals, what was seen as the adoption of the Nazi policy of bombing civilians was regarded as a major military as well as moral error. Only a handful of experts held that strategic bombing was a British invention, central to the existence of the Royal Air Force, and to British strategy in the 1930s and the early years of the war. Neither the significance nor the implications of this argument were sufficiently grasped by historians. This was in part because the standard story insisted that pre-war British aviation was weak, distorted by imperial concerns, held back by a pacifist electorate, not sufficiently promoted by governments indifferent to the requirements of modernity, and so on. All these arguments were almost inversions of reality, at least in my account, in which British aviation of the 1930s, like that of all major nations, was overwhelmingly military, was strong, was strengthened by the demands of empire, and was central to the peculiarly modern war-fighting strategy of the British state, both within the Empire and outside it. British anti-militarism, wrongly taken to be pacifism, in fact encouraged aviation, alongside other alternatives to conscript armies.

An alternative picture of England's relationship with the aeroplane required a new account of how the aeroplane was understood in England. My argument, too diffusely made, perhaps, was that a liberal-internationalist, and thus anti-nationalist and anti-fascist ideology, was fundamental to British enthusiasm for the aeroplane, and for bombing, from the interwar years. This was counter-intuitive for a number of reasons. The first was that historians, far from noting the existence of enthusiasm for the bomber, stressed fear of the bomber as the key British attitude in the 1930s, a fear which originated in the qualities of the aeroplane, and the particular geographical isolation of Britain which the aeroplane now rendered useless. Secondly, enthusiasm for aviation, and the bomber in particular, was associated by historians (as it was by some in the 1930s) with fascists and ultra-nationalists, with Nazi Germany and fascist Italy. Thirdly, there was the idea (very strong after 1945) that liberal internationalists were pacifists, naive believers in world peace and disarmament.

In fact liberal internationalists saw great dangers in the rise of nationalism and militarism. They sought to counter these enemies of liberalism not only by collective security, but also with modern machines, particularly aeroplanes, which they associated with a possible world organization charged with defending a liberal world order (one which was foreshadowed, some thought, in the British Empire itself). What I called 'liberal militarism' placed machines at the centre of British strategy, as a way of challenging larger opponents and of limiting the militarization of British society. For Britain's enemies it meant the death of civilians as a deliberate act of war.

The liberal view of the aeroplane (as I identified it) had many elements. Aeroplanes were seen as civilian inventions. That is to say they originated with civilians and had the primary purpose of civilian transportation; they were machines for (long-distance) communication which crossed political and geographical barriers. In doing so they realized liberal internationalist dreams of free trade and peace. Although the term 'global village' was not used, the idea that the aeroplane was bringing about a smaller world – shrinking time and space – was a standard cliché. This is not to say that the role of aircraft in war was not recognized, far from it, but it is to say that the power of aeroplanes in war derives from their character as world-transforming *civilian* wonders of modern science. They were thus seen as immensely powerful, transforming war completely, civilianizing and industrializing it. Aeroplanes were also weapons which, in the hands of a world authority, could bring the world to its liberal senses.

While the idea of the international air police is long forgotten, the basic assumptions of the liberal view proved to be highly influential in the ways the history of aviation is thought about. In histories of technology and industry they appear under transportation. In museums of science and technology they are central, again as transportation. While tanks and guns do not appear in such museums, aeroplanes do. Only in war museums do aeroplanes stand alongside other weapons. In histories of production, even war production, aeroplanes are seen as the product of civilian industry; histories of the aircraft industry emphasize the civilian markets for aircraft. In relation to war, they are seen as fundamental in bringing war to civilians for the first time. The Blitz fits perfectly into this narrative.

The whole historiography of industry, technology and war (which came together in academic form in the 1980s), was based on a complex of ideas of a similar sort: civilian machines and industries had transformed the nature of war from the outside. *England and the Aeroplane* challenged this interpretation, insisting on the military character of the industry: throughout the century in the key nations, military demand was very significantly greater than civil. Aeroplanes were, and to a considerable extent still are, primarily weapons of war, designed by competing nation states for national purposes. I emphasized that twentieth-century war involved militarization, rather than the civilianization so many accounts assumed. This reconsideration paralleled that undertaken by historical sociologists in the 1980s who pointed to the inadequacies of liberal and Marxist accounts of war, but went further in showing how historical accounts were deeply affected by liberal assumptions about the character and supposed origins of what were taken to be the key machines of war.

*

England and the Aeroplane also established a series of connections between enthusiasm for aviation and the ultra-right in Britain that had been systematically forgotten from the war onwards. Enthusiasm for Hitler and Mussolini was often associated with enthusiasm for aeroplanes, even if enthusiasm for aeroplanes only rarely implied enthusiasm for fascism. From the leader of the British Union of Fascists, Oswald Mosley, to important conservative politicians and press lords of the hard right like Lords Londonderry and Rothermere, enthusiasms for aviation and fascism were closely linked. Furthermore, the aircraft industry and its leaders were surprisingly often committed to hard-right positions. The important aeronautical magazine, *The Aeroplane*, was edited by a rabid anti-semite and pro-Nazi. All this was deeply problematic for a national narrative in which the aeroplane is presented as the key anti-Nazi machine, particularly of course the fighter, and it was quickly wiped from the record, even though some of the personalities were not.

That the political right was interested in the promotion of new machines and new sciences was a central theme of *England and the Aeroplane*. While obviously far from surprising in the context of twentieth-century European or world history, this thesis was novel in the British context. Here there was a powerful assumption that what technocratic impulse there was came from the left, that the right was either traditionalist or liberal, and in either case not enthused by the possibility of new machines and new knowledge. Yet, as I argued, the powerful connection between the political right and enthusiasm for machines needed to be grasped in order to make sense of the broader political history of British machines. Alas, I was not aware that Britain's most famous aeronautical engineers, Frank Whittle and Barnes Wallis, ended up on the extreme right in the 1960s.

The link between aviation and the right was central for this book's analysis of the post Second World War years. Firstly I challenged a right-wing aeronautical myth that British governments were slow or stupid in supporting aviation. But I also challenged the left account which saw post-war industry and technology policy through the framework of a moment of technological enthusiasm in the 1960s, the 'white heat' that quickly dissipated to a dull pink. I argued instead that the 'white heat' was a challenge to the technological priorities of the right. Politics mattered.

I have added a discussion of some of the recent literature to the bibliographic essay, but here I will make some general comments. Especially since the election of New Labour in 1997, decline lost its salience and among historians there was a shift in interest from the supposed phenomenon of decline. Britannia was now cool, and the economy, many thought, had been sorted by neo-liberalism. In any case historians had from the 1980s turned away from the study of the economy, business, labour, the state; cultural histories which focused on what was seen as a problematic national identity flourished. Yet many of the assumptions that had been central to declinist histories – about the nature of the elite, say –

went unchallenged in this literature, and indeed were reinforced. Declinism had entered deep into the understanding of historians and was not disposed of by ignoring the economy. That said, the last fifteen years or so have seen a transformation in our understanding of British history in many dimensions; declinism is now treated as part of that history, rather than being the lens through which history was seen. The politics of the military and of machines have become more complex in the twenty years since *England and the Aeroplane* was written and this is reflected in the fact that the identification of political position and subject matter is less marked than it was; both left and right have broadened their interests. The quality of work on British aviation and its meanings has gone up by leaps and bounds. British history has begun to look very different.

Many of the least commented on aspects of this book have, I am delighted to say, attracted attention recently. There have been many cultural histories of aviation but they have been interested mainly in what were taken to be deviant forms of aeronautical enthusiasm, and took liberal internationalist clichés about the power of aeroplanes to shrink the world and transform war as descriptions of what was happening. *England and the Aeroplane* saw these ideas as profoundly ideological and misleading about aeronautical reality. Now liberal internationalist ideas are being taken much more seriously, including in relation to thinking about aviation, and machines more generally. Equally, more attention is being given to the British right and its interest in aviation and in modern machines, not least in connection with Empire. In many different ways, indeed, twentieth-century Britain is being seen as a modern place, and its modernizers have been identified not just with liberalism and socialism, but also with conservatism and reaction. Empire too is taken seriously, not least in connection with aviation, and with science and invention more generally.

There are some areas where on reflection some gentle critics of *England and the Aeroplane* have been right, and where alas there is still much work to be done. There is much more about the personal and political networks between the aircraft industry, government and the forces to explore, not least in the way they encouraged the aeroplane to be specifically English, and indeed so connected to London and its environs. Secondly, I didn't give enough attention to the impact of the United States on Britain and on British aviation, from the early 1950s in particular. I didn't mention the stationing of vast numbers of US aircraft on Airstrip One (George Orwell's memorable name for these islands in *Nineteen Eighty-Four*), nor the support the US gave to funding the British aircraft industry.

The text is reproduced here essentially as originally published. I have made some small corrections, the most significant of which is a change in my understanding of strategic bombing – I had underrated its effects on German war production. I have reduced the unnecessary use of quotation marks, and in the bibliographic essay I have where necessary amended the titles of publications. I have also added to this essay a section on the subsequent literature on the topic. My thanks to those who have commented over the years on this book, and to Katharina Hoffmann, Herbert Mehrtens and Silke Wenk, for inviting me to reflect back on it at a conference on Myths, Gender and the Military Conquest of Air and Sea in Oldenburg in April 2009. I thank Octavia Lamb for her work on the illustrations and Jane Birdsell for her exemplary copy-editing. Special thanks are due to my agent, Clare Alexander, and to Simon Winder for his energizing enthusiasm for this book.

London, 2012

Preface to First Edition

Most books on aeroplanes focus on machines and heroics, abstracted from social, economic or political contexts. Most histories of modern England focus on the politics of welfare and on the failings of English industry and technology. This essay does neither. I present aeroplanes as a central and revealing aspect of modern English history and I see in this history not a *welfarist* nation lacking interest in technology, but a warfare state which gives a remarkably high priority to technological development. In a reversal of received wisdom, I show that English aviation and the aircraft industry were strong throughout this century – before the Great War, through the interwar years, and since the Second World War. This strength derived from the vital place of technology, industry and economic thinking within the grand designs of English strategy, and not least from English enthusiasm for the aeroplane. There was also an important political dimension. Enthusiasm for aircraft was commonly, but not exclusively, a right-wing phenomenon. This book, then, focuses on technology, industry and business, on the warfare state rather than the welfare state, and on the right rather than the left.

In the popular view England is depicted as a nation slow in supporting aviation. In 1914 the England which faced Germany was aeronautically deficient, though it created aircraft second to none during the war. In the interwar years the liberal internationalism of the electorate and of politicians, the stinginess of the Treasury and the technological conservatism of the Air Ministry ensured that by the 1930s England was peculiarly weak in the air. There were, however, individuals, firms and aeroplanes which bucked the trend: in particular Winston Churchill, and Vickers Supermarine with its Schneider Trophy-winning seaplane and Spitfire. As a result, in the summer of 1940, the Royal Air Force was able to hold off the Luftwaffe. Thus the Battle of Britain becomes the story of the Few, the island nation standing alone, the close-run-thing, the muddling-through, the boffins who made it all possible. In the autumn and the winter of 1940–41 the story shifts from the heroism and suffering of the Few to that of the Many in the Blitz of London and the provincial industrial centres and ports. The frightfulness of the Nazis committed the people to victory, the discovery of the condition of the working class led to the welfare state. England is seen as a put-upon nation, which rose to collective industrial, technological and social genius in adversity. By contrast, the post-war history is one of disappointment: it was a story of grandiose projects gone wrong – the Brabazon, the Blue Streak, the TSR2, the Concorde.

My alternative account is very different. I emphasize English enthusiasm, indeed over-enthusiasm, for the aeroplane, though to many people the idea that England was enthusiastic about any technology will appear perverse. Once we look in detail, however, it is strength rather than weakness which stands out. For example, in proportion to the size of its armed forces, Britain had the strongest air services in August 1914. In the 1920s England's aircraft industry was the largest in the world; in 1940 it out-produced Germany by 50 per cent; and well into the 1970s Britain was the third largest producer of aircraft after the United States and the Soviet Union. The primary role of the interwar Royal Air Force was strategic bombing: indeed, it attacked Germany from May 1940, months before both the Battle of Britain and the Blitz. The bombing of Britain may have stimulated the reorganization of social services, but the growth of the welfare state was also promoted by the need to employ labour on a huge scale, not least in aircraft factories. We remember the bombing of Britain, but tend to forget just how many people were involved in making, maintaining and flying aeroplanes. Bomber Command's own wartime death toll was close to that of British civilians. As for the post-war years, it is not the cancellations which are significant, but the enormous sums of money that were spent on the development of new aircraft. Thus, to rewrite the history of English aeroplanes is to rewrite important chapters in the history of England.

But the case for treating England and the aeroplane together is stronger than this. Aeroplanes and aircraft industries everywhere have been the creations of particular states; they were not autonomous developments to which states were forced to respond. We tend to see aircraft, like other important technologies, as essentially civil in origin, even when their military uses are recognized. Aircraft appear as technologies of communication and of individual freedom, transcending the artificial barriers created by states. But aircraft, I argue, have been fundamentally a military technology, created by armed services and governments for national purposes. Thus, while the standard view of England and the aeroplane is that both are liberal, civil, and anti-militaristic, my view is that the commitment of England to the aeroplane exemplifies a commitment to armed force, science, technology and industry. This contradicts the dominant image of England as anti-scientific, anti-technological, anti-industrial, and anti-militaristic.

The primary context for the study of the development of aviation is English grand strategy which, I suggest, cannot be understood in the usual schemes of political history. With some notable exceptions, it cannot be read off from the policies of political parties, much less from public opinion. In this it differs from policy towards trade unions and for welfare, though perhaps not as much as one would like to think. I see the basic strategy of the English state as one of relying on technology as a substitute for manpower, and using the technology to attack enemy civil populations and industry, rather than armies. I label this *liberal militarism*, a term I use as an aid to analysis, as an 'ideal type' of warfare. Liberal militarism had important repercussions for the structure and character of the English state and of English science, technology and industry. The specialist branches of service ministries and specialist supply ministries were manned by officials who differed radically from our image of the English civil servant: they were staffed by serving officers, scientific, technological and industrial experts, rather than generalist amateurs eschewing action for the quiet life. They intervened in selected industries and funded a very considerable proportion of the national scientific and technological effort before, as well as after, the Second World War.

The central concern of the literature on England and technology in the twentieth century is the failure of English technology and the consequent 'decline' of the economy. As a consequence of this *declinist* emphasis, the best known facts about English science, technology and industry in the twentieth century appear to be the division between 'the Two Cultures', the 'low status of engineers', and the anti-industrial orientation of the English elite. These facts are granted great explanatory power not only in accounts of the economic decline, but also in the history of armament development and production. In fact, our historical understanding of the place of science and technology in twentieth-century England is rudimentary, but not just because historians ignore technology. Unfortunately historians have tended to write Whig histories of science and technology, that is histories which take the present as the reference point and ignore historical developments which are not immediately obvious as historical precursors. Such an approach distorts the historical record in itself, but the historiography of twentieth-century English science and technology is further confused by a modern English vice I call *inverted Whiggism*. Unlike the original optimistic Whig history it does not look for early examples of parliamentary democracy and the decencies of England; instead, it dredges up any old example of a civil servant being ignorant of technology, a businessman not investing in a modern machine, or a soldier doubting the efficacy of new weapons. The inverted Whig historians of science and technology have been at work for about a hundred years; their prodigious industry has produced an impressive pile of horrors.

Given that we have so much evidence, it might seem rash to challenge the picture of the English elite as anti-scientific and anti-industrial, of English business as congenitally short-sighted, or of the English people trapped in an idiotic longing for all things rural. But if we do accept these accounts we face a very serious historical problem. How do we explain the fact that English industrial output, as well as scientific and technological output, have increased dramatically since 1880? The explanations of the declinists too often turn out to be explanations not of relatively slow growth but of an imagined stagnation or even absolute decline. They are, in other words, a historiographical sledge-hammer to crack a historical nut; impressive, but pointless. Just like, one is tempted to add, much English technology.

But the case against the declinist historiography is stronger still. In the declinist literature there is an implicit blueprint for modernization: long-term, technocratic administration, large firms, lots of R & D, and a culture suffused with celebratory accounts of scientists, engineers and industrialists. The declinists often imagine that Other

Countries, to use E. P. Thompson's phrase, had these features, but they are blind to their existence in England. For they did exist, at least in connection with the aeroplane. This case cannot be dismissed as exceptional, for the histories of England and the aeroplane have been closely intertwined. Many English writers wrote about them, and more English gentlemen flew them; English engineers designed them, and English governments paid them to do it; English industry made huge numbers of them, and many more of England's enemies were killed by them. However, commitment to scientific, technological and industrial solutions to defence and economic problems is not in itself a guarantee of success (nor is the converse true).

Defence issues, and above all scientific and technological issues, are usually seen as 'bottom line' subjects, close to reality. Analysts of these matters, now as in the past, pride themselves on their realism and display their contempt of politics and the delusions of the mass: they deal in facts not theories, crude realities rather than dreams. No-nonsense analysis of the English condition was a growth industry in the 1980s; the cruel real world was invoked, like an avenging God, to crush do-gooders, wimps, wets and socialists. The view that such analysts put forward, that the English have been anti-militaristic, anti-scientific, anti-technological and anti-industrial, has been widely accepted, even by those who were accused of these sins. But no-nonsense analysts were and are just as capable of talking nonsense as anyone else.

Unfortunately, however, neither the history of war nor the history of science, technology and industry tend to be seen in their political and ideological context. The consequence is that we cower before self-appointed realistic tough guys without questioning their authority. To see war, science, technology and industry as issues over which there can be legitimate disagreement and debate is as important for democracy as universal suffrage.

One important barrier to a proper debate about these topics is the failure of most historians to see even the rhetoric of science and technology as political and ideological. Another, just as significant but more surprising, is that the history of English warfare is the preserve of the right. The English left has studied the history of opposition to war rather than the history of war, and indeed the politics of the left rather than those of the right. Socialist historians tend to prefer the history of the people, of everyday life, of the back-to-back rather than the country-house, of the workplace rather than the Court, of the down-trodden rather than the courtier. Conservative historians prefer the history of 'high' politics, war and diplomacy, and many want schoolchildren to be taught nationalistic chronicles of Britain and Britishness – well, England and Englishness – Kings and Queens, Parliament, and Wars. Professor Skidelsky, justifiably, summed up the difference between these positions by asking whether the Battle of Britain was more important than the creation of the National Health Service.

There is, however, nothing inevitable about such an alignment of political sympathy and subject matter. After all, it is not difficult to imagine a national and patriotic history of the English working class stressing deference to King and Country, addiction to beer and horse racing and suspicion of foreigners. Indeed, it exists in the work of G. M. Trevelyan. Neither is it difficult to imagine a socialist account of the English nation and nationalism, of the Monarchy, the constitution and war. Marx and Engels, after all, wrote more about legal, political and military history than about the domestic habits of English working subjects. Tom Nairn's study of the Monarchy is a more recent example. My book, while endorsing the view that the waging of aeronautical war is central to English history, also seeks to show that the relationship of England to the aeroplane is too serious a business to be left to the historiographical right.

To conclude, two points need to be made. The first concerns terminology – the use of the word 'England' in my title. The statistics I use are for Great Britain or the United Kingdom. I am aware that many of the protagonists in this story are not English, and that many who served in the RAF, in the Second World War especially, were not English either. But it remains the case that aeroplanes were associated with England rather than Scotland, Wales or Northern Ireland. Indeed, the heart of the association lay in the Home Counties, with the sort of 'Englishness' that foreigners usually understand. Tom Nairn, in an erudite continental joke, used the term 'Ukania' to describe this thing we all know but cannot precisely name. The Battle of Britain is a Home Counties affair; the Blitz is largely a Cockney story, in both fact and fiction.

Furthermore, the aircraft industry was English: it was created and grew in the South of England and only spread to Scotland, Ireland and Wales in wartime. The scientific and technological resources on which the industry drew were also largely English.

The second point concerns the relationship between this book and the academic literature on the topics it covers. It will be obvious that this is an essay rather than a historical monograph. It is short, with a high ratio of assertion to detailed evidence, and with relatively little commentary on previous authors. I make no apology for this: my primary aim has been to tell a straightforward and brief story about England and the aeroplane. To do this I was forced to challenge what I see as the conventional picture of England and the aeroplane, which permeates both the academic and popular literature. Such an approach carries dangers, in particular of wrongly generalizing about the 'conventional picture', about particular literatures, political positions, and so on. Of course, not all historians of twentieth-century English science and technology are declinists, just as not all socialist historians ignore warfare and the state. In a longer and different book these qualifications would be carefully noted. There is, however, a strong case for making such generalizations: they help us to understand. They have helped me to appreciate why historians have written as they have on England and the aeroplane, and why my alternative story has not been told before; I hope they will help the reader also. The extent to which this essay appears rhetorical and polemical is, I hope, no more than a reflection of the power of the covert polemic and rhetoric of the conventional story.

In writing a book such as this many debts are incurred. Those due to the authors of books and articles on the English state and English aviation are acknowledged in the notes and especially in the bibliography. But learning is not just a matter of reading; it involves teachers, friends, colleagues and students. Allan Chapman of the University of Oxford started me off as a historian; Gary Werskey, my Ph.D. supervisor, worked on still refractory material with care and enthusiasm. This book has been written in the Centre for the History of Science, Technology and Medicine in the University of Manchester, where I have the good fortune to be able to escape, as far as that is possible, from the cruel real world of a decaying university system. I must thank John Pickstone for that, and also Richard Coopey, Roger Cooter, Mary Fissell, Jonathan Harwood, Simon Lee, Bill Luckin, James Small and Steve Sturdy (who suggested the term 'liberal militarism' to me). Friends in other departments and other universities, especially Paul Heywood, Kirsty Hughes, Frankie Lynch, Brendan O'Leary, and Richard Whittington, have over the years been a vital source of inspiration and support. I would also like to thank Helen Andrews, Bharat Bhushan, Neil McCartney, Chris Mitchell, Jim Rennie, Helen Roberts and Jenny Thompson. Wing Commander Geoffrey Bennett, John Pickstone and Jim Rennie kindly commented on the nearly-finished text; I am grateful too to an anonymous referee. Bill Luckin, Joan Mottram and John Pickstone very generously helped copy-edit the text at a late stage. Finally, I would like to thank the Manchester and Salford Universities' Air Squadron who very kindly used a Bulldog trainer to make an ephemeral godling out of a groundling, and Alex Robertson who first suggested I should write a book on the aircraft industry.

Manchester, 1990

1. The Strange Birth of Aeronautical England

The story of the birth of powered, controlled flight has been told many times. The achievements of the Wright brothers, and of the European pioneers, provide endless material for books, films and even specialist monthly magazines. For our purposes we do not need to retell these tales, but it is necessary to highlight certain neglected themes. The first is the importance not just of practical experience but of academic science; the second the commercial impulse present from the beginning; the third the connection between the birth of aviation and the armament race between the major powers before 1914. Science, money, politics and war were in there at the beginning.

The Montgolfier brothers, the eighteenth-century inventors of the hot-air balloon, were French provincials who believed, in their practical way, that their balloon was pushed up into the air by the fiery principle in smoke. The Parisian scientific elite responded within months to what it saw as a challenge by the discredited Aristotelian physics. To refute the Ancients they had a gas balloon made using hydrogen, which like hot air was lighter than air, to demonstrate it was lightness and not the principle of fire that caused the balloon to rise. In the nineteenth century two engineers from Chard, Somerset, wanted to make a flying steam engine. One, William Henson, patented his

'Aerial Steam Carriage' and attempted to incorporate his 'Aerial Transit Company' in 1842. The required Parliamentary Bill was laughed out. Even earlier in the nineteenth century the English natural philosopher Sir George Cayley, 6th baronet, had done largely theoretical work on mechanical flight; his coachman is reputed to have made a short flight in a glider of his master's design. Cayley's scientific friends formed the Aeronautical Society in 1866, nine years after his death. By the late nineteenth century there was sustained scientific experimentation with gliders by, for example, Otto Lilienthal in Germany and Percy Pilcher, a lecturer in engineering at the University of Glasgow. In the United States, the land of the heroic inventor, we find that from 1898 the War Department was financing the aeronautical researches of Samuel Pierpont Langley, the Secretary of the Smithsonian Institution, an academic astronomer.

The Wright brothers were the first to achieve controlled, powered flight, a feat performed in December 1903. According to legend they were merely practical men who, in the American way, became unassuming heroes. But if they were practical men they were also pioneer experimenters. Their first powered flight in 1903 was one of a long series of experiments and test flights designed to create a usable flying machine. They also experimented using wind tunnels and avidly read, and contributed to, the developing technical literature on aviation. There were still plenty of cranks, opportunists and self-publicists involved in promoting aeronautical schemes of all kinds. Then, as now, people threw themselves off the ends of piers with feathers strapped to their arms; then, as now, routine and careful experimentation led to new developments in aviation. But in one interesting way the Wright brothers combined the approaches of the engineer and the crank: they sought human mastery of the air rather than its mastery by machine. What distinguished first their gliders and then their powered flyers from those of other pioneers was that they were sensitively controllable extensions of the human pilot: the Wright brothers were not only the first successful engineers of flight, they were also the first pilots.

Although often portrayed as humble bicycle makers, the Wrights were shrewd businessmen. If their pioneering flight of 1903, and subsequent flights until 1908, were not as well known as they are today, it was not because they lived in a backwater, or were innocent of the ways of the world. On the contrary, they saw their invention as a potential money-spinner, and did not want prying eyes about; they wanted to perfect their flying machine and sell it to the highest bidder. They were not just in aviation to make history, they also wanted to make money, and making money meant selling aircraft to the world's armies and navies. They were fortunate in that key military figures were quick to see the importance of aviation. Just months after the Wrights' first successful flight they were visited by Colonel J. E. Capper, the head of ballooning in the British Army. A year later the Wrights offered their flyer and associated technical knowledge to the British War Office (Army Ministry); by late 1905 they had established contacts with the American and French governments.

By the spring of 1906 they had added Germany, Italy, Russia, Austria and Japan to their list. But the major problem, as the British soon found, was not the price they put on their invention, but the fact that the Wrights would not allow the British military attaché to see the flyer in operation until a contract had been signed! In December 1906 the War Office rejected the Wright flyer. In 1907 the Wright brothers decided to go professional and appointed Charles R. Flint as their negotiator with foreign governments. Flint was a well-known arms dealer, connected to the banking houses of Rothschild and Morgan, and a friend of Theodore Roosevelt. He was an ambitious and vigorous salesman who decided to sell not single aircraft but whole air forces: 50 flyers at £2,000 each! The War Ministries and Chancelleries of the Old World were enticed by agents, communicating in code with Flint. Flint's 'merchant of death' in London, Lady Jane Taylor, worked assiduously on the Secretary of State for War (Army Minister), R. B. Haldane, on the First Lord of the Admiralty (Navy Minister), Lord Tweedmouth, and on Lord Northcliffe, who would soon be using his *Daily Mail* to great effect in promoting aviation. Female aristocrats and the *Daily Mail* will appear again in our story.

English Aviation

Haldane and Tweedmouth rejected these advances – more appropriate, it might seem, to a 1930s spy film set in a Balkan capital. However, the English had their own aeronautical effort which, like Lady Taylor's approaches, was highly unorthodox. From 1906 an American showman and illiterate playwright, Samuel Cody, was engaged in experiments on gliders and powered flight for the Army Balloon Factory. Cody dressed like his famous namesake 'Buffalo Bill' Cody and had his white horse fed at the expense of the Army. He would make the first powered ascent in Britain in October 1908, in an aircraft suspiciously like the Wright flyer. The first powered flight in Europe, in October 1906, had been made in France by another representative of the New World: the Brazilian Santos Dumont. But Old World inventors too were trying their hand: at the Balloon Factory with Cody was Lieutenant J. W. Dunne, who shamelessly exploited his family connections with the Army to keep his experiments going. The lowly lieutenant also had a direct line to Haldane, through H. G. Wells, a mutual friend. It was with Dunne's advice that Wells wrote his 1908 bestseller *The War in the Air.*

In 1908 the Wright brothers first demonstrated their flyer in France, where it easily outflew its European, largely French, competitors. It was already clear what these aircraft were for: as Northcliffe's representative telegraphed to London: 'Aeroplane primarily intended war machine stop . . .'[1] Northcliffe himself went to see the Wright flyer and dragged the leader of the opposition, A. J. Balfour, to see it too. It was in this context that the British government moved to develop a new aeronautical policy, well before Blériot made his famous flight across the Channel and had his aeroplane exhibited at Selfridges on

Oxford Street, next to the 'Departments of Sports, Motor Requisites and Motor Clothing'. The years from 1908 to 1914 were years of rapid advance in English aviation, but also of much debate and controversy: between the Army and the Navy; between the advocates of a 'scientific' and a 'practical' approach; and about the respective roles of the private and public sectors. These arguments and rivalries were indicative of the importance given to aviation.

In late 1908 the Prime Minister, Herbert Asquith, referred the question of 'Aerial Navigation' to the Committee of Imperial Defence (CID), a very high-powered committee established after the Boer War to co-ordinate the policies of the War Office, Admiralty and the state as a whole. It was both a think-tank and a ministerial and official committee. Indeed, R. B. Haldane, the Secretary of State for War between 1906 and 1911, and the most intellectual of Edwardian politicians, was a great enthusiast for the CID, and it was he who had the most direct impact on aviation policy. Richard Haldane was a philosopher by training, a barrister by profession, and a cunning and successful politician. In his philosophy he was a Hegelian, in his politics he was a liberal imperialist and the leading political enthusiast for educational and scientific progress. He was one of the central figures in the expansion of English university education in the Edwardian years, and was President of the major pro-science lobby, the British Science Guild. Just as he set out to create a 'Hegelian' army, he aimed to develop aviation policy and aeronautics on a rational, scientific basis.

Haldane regarded the investigations into powered

flight by Cody and Dunne as not properly scientific, and he sacked them both in 1909; the head of the Balloon Factory was transferred to other duties. In their place, Haldane brought in a well-known consulting engineer, Mervyn O'Gorman, to head what was renamed the Army Aircraft Factory. He also established an Advisory Committee on Aeronautics (ACA), which reported to the Prime Minister, and was headed by Britain's most distinguished physicist, and Balfour's brother-in-law, Lord Rayleigh. Rayleigh was no stranger to the Army: he had chaired the high-level War Office Explosives Committee a few years previously. The ACA was made up of scientists, engineers, and senior representatives of the Army and Navy. Its job was to advise the government on aeronautical research and oversee the research at the Aircraft Factory and at the National Physical Laboratory (NPL), which began aerodynamic research in 1909. The ACA, under the titles Aeronautical Research Committee and then Council, continued in existence until 1980.

From the very beginning the ACA was strongly linked to the academic community. There was a substantial tradition of academic engineering in the universities, much of it very relevant to aeronautics. Manchester was an important centre for such work. The Professor of Mathematics, Horace Lamb, wrote a classic book on hydrodynamics, and later advised the air authorities. Osborne Reynolds, Professor of Engineering, did vital fundamental work in fluid mechanics. His successor in the (industrially funded) chair of engineering, J. E. Petavel, was appointed to the ACA at its inception. It was in Edwardian Manchester that the young Ludwig Wittgenstein studied aeronautical engineering. At the University of Cambridge, Lord Rayleigh had made fundamental contributions to fluid dynamics. The head of the Engineering Department, Bertram Hopkinson, was to head aeronautical research in the war. His predecessor, Alfred Ewing, had become Director of Naval Education at the Admiralty. The Cambridge Engineering School was the largest producer of graduate engineers in the country, and its graduates were particularly well trained in the complex mathematics which aerodynamic research required.

The staff of both the NPL and the Factory came to be dominated by graduate engineers from Cambridge. B. M. Jones, for example, left Cambridge in 1909, spent two years at the Woolwich Arsenal, then went to the NPL as an Imperial College research student, before joining the armament firm Armstrong-Whitworth. In 1914 he went to Farnborough, where he was joined by other young Cambridge engineers including E. T. Busk, W. S. Farren, R. McKinnon Wood, and R. H. Mayo, as well as scientists like Frederick Lindemann, G. I. Taylor and Frederick Aston. Other pre-1914 Cambridge engineers who became famous in the aeronautical world were the Hon. C. S. Rolls, Harry Ricardo and H. E. Wimperis. Engineers trained in other universities provided a much smaller number of famous aeronautical figures. Examples are A. A. Griffiths (Liverpool), F. B. Halford (Nottingham), Robert Blackburn (Leeds), and A. V. Roe (King's College, London).

Haldane's commitment to a scientific approach may

seem to be so obvious as to merit no comment. In the many popular works extolling the wonders of modern science which have appeared this century the aeroplane is seen as a dramatic confirmation of the power of science. As we have seen, the science of flight and the practice of flight developed together. But it is important to remember that flight did not come wholly out of the laboratory: the first powered aircraft flew in real air, not a perfect gas, and was flown by men who understood this. Indeed there was a debate as to whether aircraft should be developed 'practically' or 'scientifically'. The debate was much more than an academic dispute between different philosophies of progress: it was concerned also with the balance between public and private effort and between the concentration and diffusion of effort.

Haldane's view that, as he put it in the first Parliamentary debate on aviation (in 1909), 'Science should come first'[2] was challenged by Arthur Lee, MP, chairman of the Parliamentary Aerial Defence Committee:

> The right hon. gentleman I know, is much enamoured of, I will not say hypnotized by, the blessed word 'Science', but while pure science is very well in its way, I think this is a case where it is of more value when diluted by a great deal of practical experience.[3]

The pioneer manufacturers and their supporters also espoused a 'practical' approach, which for them meant many designers and engineers designing many different types in competition with each other. Historians of aviation have tended to support them: Malcolm Cooper has regretted that 'air policy came to revolve around state-controlled investigation of the science of aeronautics, at the expense of the subsidization of private entrepreneurs'.[4] Other historians have criticized the War Office by making a comparison with the policies of the Admiralty:

> The War Office lent a ready ear to the theorists and the scientific experts especially those at the Royal Aircraft Factory, and was all in favour of standardization. The Admiralty adopted the sounder principle of listening to what the pilots said, and giving the pilots what they wanted, whilst at the same time experimenting freely with any aeroplane which appeared to have possibilities, whatever its source of origin and whether the civil servants at Farnborough approved of it or not.[5]

But such arguments and contrasts can be misleading. The Farnborough staff were not all theorists: Mervyn O'Gorman was a consulting engineer, and he recruited young and ambitious designers as well as the university graduates mentioned earlier. Geoffrey de Havilland, who first flew in late 1909 in a plane designed by himself, met O'Gorman and sold his plane to the War Office for £400, joining Farnborough to superintend its development and build new machines.[6] From 1912 his assistant was H. P. Folland, who had been an apprentice with the Lanchester Motor Company and had worked at the Swift and Daimler car companies. Frederick Green was also recruited from Daimler. All three would be prominent in the private industry in the interwar years: two would found aircraft firms bearing their names.

Furthermore, despite its name, the amount of production undertaken by the Factory was minimal. In June 1914, for example, the Army had contracts for 122 aircraft, of which only twenty-four were to be built by the Factory. In other words most of the aircraft ordered by the Army were built by private manufacturers, including the large armourers Coventry Ordnance Works, Vickers and Armstrong-Whitworth. However, of the aircraft to be built by private firms, twenty-five were private designs, eighty-one were Factory designs and sixteen were French designs.[7] But although more aircraft were built to Factory designs than private designs, the number of privately designed types was greater than the number of Factory-designed types. In other words the Army, like the Admiralty, was subsidizing private design as well as relying on private manufacturers for production.

Nevertheless there was a real difference between the approaches to aeronautical development of the scientifically minded civil servants and the more practical private firms. The scientific approach to aircraft development was exemplified by the BE2c, a two-seater reconnaissance plane, which was remarkable for the fact that it was a properly stable aircraft. It was the product of long researches at Farnborough and the NPL into flight stability, drawing on the work of the Cambridge-trained mathematician and Professor of Pure and Applied Mathematics at Bangor, G. H. Bryan, who had produced a theory of stable flight in 1911. In tests the BE2c flew between sixty and seventy miles with rudder control only: a remarkable achievement.

At the outbreak of war the War Office decided to place particularly large orders for the BE2c, which as a result dominated aircraft output for the first year of the war. There were good reasons for this decision. The Factory could produce good engineering drawings to give to experienced and inexperienced firms alike; standardization also greatly aided quality control. But as it turned out, the BE2c, although an excellent reconnaissance machine, was not suitable for fighting. Its stability in flight was necessarily bought at the expense of manoeuvrability, and when the Germans introduced the highly unstable but very manoeuvrable Fokker fighters in 1915, BE2cs were shot down in large numbers. This led to a campaign against the Army's Royal Flying Corps (RFC) and the Factory, and to a judicial enquiry into the RFC, which ended design at Farnborough. O'Gorman was forced to resign. Most of his designers resigned as well and went to the private aircraft industry. The private manufacturers had been very hostile to Farnborough; even twenty years later Frederick Handley Page would say that 'the BE2c, a government design, was completely outclassed by a privately produced aircraft on the other side'.[8] This judgement was unfair: the BE2c performed its task very well, and continued in production to the end of the war. Furthermore, many Factory-designed aircraft of different types, as well as engines, continued to be produced during the war in large numbers. For example, in 1917 and 1918 the Factory-designed SE5, with the Sopwith Camel and de Havilland's (he had left the factory in 1914) Airco DH9 dominated production, over 5,000 of the first two types being produced. But the success of this and other designs did not save the Factory: the English state never designed aircraft again.

Manufacturers, Markets and Strategy

Between 1908 and 1914 a great number of private firms were set up to design and manufacture aircraft. A number started by building French designs, for example, Claude Graham-White's firm at Hendon. The majority, however, were firms established by young engineers and aviators to build their own designs, for example T. O. M. Sopwith (1911), Frederick Handley Page (1908), Robert Blackburn (1910), Noel Pemberton Billing (1913) and A. V. Roe (1910). Not all the pioneering businesses survived as producers, but their founders sometimes went to work for others. Thus T. Howard Wright produced his own aircraft in 1908–9, but then worked as a designer for Coventry Ordnance Works, and later J. S. White; Lieutenant J. W. Dunne worked for Blair-Atholl Aeronautical Syndicate, John Dudley North (later of Boulton Paul), started work at Horatio Barber's Aeronautical Syndicate at Hendon.

The heroic entrepreneurs and pioneering designers have received great attention in the literature. It should not be forgotten, however, that many established Edwardian firms diversified into aircraft production before the Great War. At the top of the list must come the great Edwardian armourers: Vickers, Armstrong-Whitworth, Beardmore and Coventry Ordnance Works. These huge firms were among the largest employers of manufacturing labour in the Edwardian years. Each started producing and designing aircraft before 1914. But armourers were not the only established enterprises that entered aviation in these years. Sir George White, the millionaire Bristol businessman, used the facilities of his Bristol tramway empire to found the British and Colonial Aeroplane Company in 1910, at first building French designs. The newspaper owner George Holt Thomas created the Aircraft Manufacturing Company in 1912. Holt Thomas, owner of the *Daily Graphic* and the *Graphic* (one of the great illustrated weeklies, founded in the 1860s), had already offered a £1,000 prize for aviation in 1906. He later used his extensive social and journalistic contacts to lobby for extra expenditure on military aircraft. Smaller established firms also entered aviation: the balloon builders Short Bros. started manufacture of Wright aeroplanes in 1908. Two boat-building firms, S. E. Saunders and J. S. White, also went into aircraft. The reason for diversifying into aircraft design and production is clear enough: there was a reasonable market for aircraft and every prospect of a larger one. This market was primarily a military and naval one.

It is often thought that European armies did not know what to do with aircraft in 1914, that aircraft hit them as a bolt from the blue. This argument is an example of an influential assumption that soldiers and sailors are stupid, or at least less intelligent than engineers, and that only brute circumstance would force them to accept new technology. But these stories should not be taken seriously. As has already been noted, the Army kept a close watch on the development of aviation from the beginning. In 1911 the Air Battalion of the Royal Engineers was formed. By 1912, according to the War Office, aviation was out of the experimental stage 'as regards employment in warfare'. The Italians had used aircraft in operations in Tripoli, and 'an active and progressive policy' became 'imperatively urgent'.[9] The Royal Navy, too, showed its keen interest in aircraft from around this time.

Interestingly enough, the government hoped to organize a single air corps to serve both the Army and the Navy. In 1912 it established the Royal Flying Corps, which had a military and naval wing, as well as common initial flight training at the Central Flying School on Salisbury Plain. The Army Aircraft Factory was renamed the Royal Aircraft Factory, and was intended to serve the two wings of the Corps. However, the Navy in particular did not want to lose even partial control of aviation and decided to train its own pilots at the Naval Flying School in Eastchurch and to pursue its own procurement policy. In July 1914 it secured official recognition of the existence of a separate Royal Naval Air Service (RNAS). The Royal Flying Corps remained as the Army's Flying Corps and so two air forces went to war in 1914. In August 1914 the RFC and the RNAS were both largely shore-based forces of about the same size. The RFC had sixty-three first-line aircraft and the RNAS had fifty. Between them they had 2,073 officers and men: more than half the 900 qualified British pilots were in the air services.[10]

Overall, England had fewer aircraft than the other great powers. The total of 113 compares with 120 for France, 232 for Germany, 226 for Russia and 36 for Austro-Hungary. These figures are commonly cited to indicate England's relative weakness but such a conclusion is based on the assumption that absolute air strength was important in 1914. If we consider what aircraft were for we may reach a different conclusion. Since aircraft were used for reconnaissance by both armies and navies, the number of aircraft should be considered in terms of the needs of each force. If we do this England comes out as having the most aeronautically inclined army, since its army was very much smaller than that of France, Germany or Russia. Four squadrons of the RFC flew to France to join the four divisions of the British Expeditionary Force. On 20 August the RFC spotted the advancing German army just as they were supposed to do. As far as the Navy is concerned, it had more aircraft than any other, which is not surprising given its size, but it was also probably ahead of all the major navies in aircraft intensity.

The strength of the air services should come as no surprise. England was, after all, the first industrial nation. Political economy and natural science were vitally important elements in English culture. Just as important was the fact that from the end of the nineteenth century England was challenged, industrially, commercially and militarily, by nations which were larger, and thus potentially or actually more powerful. To defend itself, and to maintain control over its markets, trade routes and Empire, England had to rely on diplomacy and on efficient and cost-effective armed services. In the late nineteenth century the Royal Navy was England's principal defensive and offensive weapon. With the rise of the German naval threat it was enlarged, modernized and increasingly deployed in the North Sea. This was an attempt to find a technological, economic and economical solution to England's strategic problems. As David French has argued:

> by August 1914 Britain intended to fight the war by blockading Germany and causing its economy to collapse. Simultaneously the Royal Navy would keep open Britain's sea lanes and so the British economy would be able to supply its allies with all the munitions they needed to carry on the land war.[11]

This technological and economic strategy failed, and England had quickly to resort first to a volunteer mass army, and then to a conscript mass army.

In the Edwardian years there was certainly opposition to reliance on a high-technology navy for the defence of the realm. While navalists stressed the economic and strategic efficiency of navalism – there was no need to have a mass army – advocates of the 'nation in arms' objected to the liberal idea of defence as an insurance policy subcontracted to sailors and machines: what mattered in war was the martial spirit and patriotic unity of the whole nation. Within the navy too, the 'historical school' favoured a return to Nelsonian principles of heroic command, rather than the '*materiel* school' road of organization and technology. Both arguments were very public: the first was encapsulated in the campaign for conscription embodied in Earl Roberts' National Service League, the second in the battle between Admiral Fisher and Lord Charles Beresford. But the battle was won by those who wanted economy in defence: a strong, technologically advanced navy and a small but well-equipped Expeditionary Force. Thus neither liberalism nor the maritime orientation of England retarded the development of defence technology: it stimulated it. We should not be surprised, then, that aeroplanes, as an important new technology, should find a prominent place in the services, or that key political figures like Balfour, Haldane and Winston Churchill were enthusiastic supporters of aviation in these years.

The popular image of Edwardian England is very different. We are invited to dwell on country houses, public schools, cricket, the Empire, the City, London and the countryside. This Edwardian England is pleasurable, effete and declining, and the subject of nostalgic reflections: the young English aesthete would end up dismembered on the barbed wire of Flanders. This Edwardian England was doomed by modernity: the Great War was a gale of creative destruction in which the liberal state was transformed into the interventionist state and the courtier politicians gave way to the hard men from the North. But as many historians have pointed out, Edwardian England should be seen as part of the twentieth century. It was, for example, much more scientific, technological and industrial than Victorian England. We forget that the cotton mills, coal mines, railways and engineering works which we tend to think of as typical of England in 1850 were much more typical of 1914 than they were of 1850, or needless to say, the Industrial Revolution proper. Neither should we forget the new technologies of the twentieth century which were already established in Edwardian England: motor-cars, photography, the cinema, the cheap press, the telephone, and electric power and light. The Royal Navy, that great symbol of Edwardian England, was probably the largest technologically oriented institution in the world, operating dreadnoughts powered by steam turbines fed by oil-fired boilers, and which communicated by wireless telegraphy.

Our image of Edwardian England and its technology is also distorted by a dubious cultural theory of 'decline'. Critics summon up *A Shropshire Lad*, Beatrix Potter and E. M. Forster and forget Conan Doyle and H. G. Wells, both famous enthusiasts for science and technology. But the level of intellectual enthusiasm for technology should not, in any case, be taken as a reflection of the level of technical development. Literary enthusiasm for technology was at its most extravagant where technical development was weak, notably in Italy and Russia. Filipo Marinetti, in his famous 1909 *Futurist Manifesto*, published in the French daily *Le Figaro*, and later in the *Observer*, heaped spirited abuse on bourgeois culture and extolled speed, heroic revolt, technology and war:

> We will glorify war – the world's only hygiene – militarism, patriotism, the destructive gesture of freedom-bringers, beautiful ideas worth dying for, and scorn for women . . . we will sing of the vibrant nightly fervour of arsenals and

> shipyards blazing with violent electric moons; greedy railway stations that devour smoke-plumed serpents; factories hung on clouds by the crooked lines of their smoke; bridges that stride the rivers like giant gymnasts, flashing in the sun with a glitter of knives; adventurous steamers that sniff the horizon; deep-chested locomotives whose wheels paw the tracks like hooves of enormous steel horses bridled by tubing; and the sleek flight of planes whose propellers chatter in the wind like banners and seem to cheer like an enthusiastic crowd.[12]

Britain had a less significant variant of Futurism: Percy Wyndham Lewis's Vorticism. Asked by his Italian homologue to declare himself a Futurist he responded: '. . . you wops insist too much on the Machine . . . We've had machines here in England for a donkey's years. They're no novelty to us'.[13] If there was anywhere that fitted Marinetti's description it was not Italy, but England.

Politics and Aviation

Aviation was, from the first, a very public technology: enthusiasts for it lobbied politicians and tried to mobilize the public. The aeronautical lobby, like the navy and army lobbies, was associated with anti-liberal politics. The right-wing press were strong supporters of aviation, and the aeronautical press was right wing. In January 1909 the Aerial League of the British Empire was formed. In April 1909 it held a joint meeting with the Aeronautical Society and the

Aero Club, where it was decided that the first would concern itself with patriotic and education matters, the second with science and the third with sport. The Aerial League of the British Empire (and a Women's Aerial League) was supported by newspapers like the *Daily Mail* and the *Morning Post*, as well as two specialist aeronautical papers, *Flight* (1909) and *The Aeroplane* (1911). The *Morning Post* also made its mark by launching an appeal to buy a foreign airship through a National Airship Fund. The Committee included Earl Roberts, Viscount Milner and Lord Charles Beresford, representing, according to *Flight*, 'martial patriotism, statesmanship and seafaring supremacy'.[14] But it was the *Daily Mail* which led the Fleet Street pack in promoting aviation: by 1914 it had paid out £24,050 in prize money for aeronautical contests, including the crossing of the English Channel.[15]

Parliament too had its aeronautical lobby, the Parliamentary Aerial Defence Committee, which was established in 1909 and which worked closely with the Aerial League. Its chairmen, successively Arthur Lee, Colonel W. Ashley and William Joynson-Hicks, kept up pressure on the Liberal government for higher spending on aviation. Before and during the war Joynson-Hicks was concerned that the War Office was not doing enough to promote aviation and he harried the unfortunate Colonel Seeley, now Secretary of State for War. In 1913 he forced the War Office to allow him and another member to count for themselves the number of aircraft in the RFC. They found that the official figures had included all sorts of aircraft in many states of repair; only about fifty-two were in flying order.[16] This was nevertheless a large number given the size of the Army.

During the First World War aeronautical politics became even more bad-tempered and controversial than it had been in peacetime. One important reason for this was that the Army and Navy air forces competed with each other over roles and particularly over increasingly limited resources for manufacturing aircraft. The growth of the air services was very rapid indeed. By the end of the war the number of personnel in the air services was ten times greater than at the beginning of the war, and there were something like fifteen times more aircraft in the first line. Towards the end of the war, to take another index, the RFC had about 12 per cent of the officer strength of the British Army, compared with 45 per cent in the infantry.

The war saw the creation of a very large aircraft industry, with increases in output accelerating through the war. Monthly output increased from about ten per month at the beginning of the war to 122 in 1917 and 2,688 in 1918. The labour force employed making aircraft engines and parts, but excluding materials, rose from nearly 49,000 in October 1916 to 154,000 in November 1917 to 268,000 in October 1918. Each of the main producers of aircraft and engines employed thousands by the end of the war: Airco, the largest, employed 7,000; Sopwith increased its employment from 200 to 3,000; Bristol reached more than 3,000; Handley Page 2,500; Blackburn 2,000; Rolls-Royce, the largest aero-engine producer, 8,000. The Vickers plant at Brooklands was turning out one tenth of all British aircraft at the end of the war. Other large firms like

Beardmore, Armstrong-Whitworth, Harland and Wolff of Belfast, and Weir of Clydeside also made aircraft on a large scale. Motor-car firms made airframes and engines: for example, Austin Motors, Daimler, Napier, Siddeley Deasy, Sunbeam, Bentley and ABC. Furniture makers were also brought in, like Boulton and Paul of Norwich; and architectural decorators, for example H. H. Martyn of Cheltenham, which with Airco formed the Gloucestershire Aircraft Company (later called Gloster Aircraft Company) in 1915. Other new producers included Fairey Aviation Company (1915) and Westland (1915). To these firms may be added a huge number of subcontractors making propellers, electrical firms supplying magnetos, chemical firms supplying 'dope', textile firms supplying canvas and firms supplying instruments and cameras.

Asquith's government attempted to bring a measure of co-ordination into air policy by the appointment of very senior politicians to oversee both air services. The Joint Air War Committee, established under Lord Derby in 1916, did not last long and was replaced by an Air Board headed by Lord Curzon. This too proved to be a failure due to the intransigence of the Navy under Balfour, which successfully resisted Curzon's attempt to take over the supply of aircraft. It was under the Lloyd George government, established in December 1916, that businessmen, rather than politicians, were brought in to try and sort out the mess. A new, strong Air Board was established under Lord Cowdray, a liberal imperialist civil engineering and oil magnate, in the Hotel Cecil on the Strand. The offices of the heads of the RFC, the RNAS and William Weir, the Scottish businessman who controlled aircraft production for the Ministry of Munitions, were also put into the hotel. Later a single Air Ministry was formed (under first Lord Rothermere, then William Weir), a single Royal Air Force, and a united design and supply organization in the Ministry of Munitions.

There certainly was an industrial logic in unifying aircraft supply, and co-ordinating it with the rest of war production through the Ministry of Munitions. The creation of a unified air service was not, however, just the result of pressures to rationalize the supply of aircraft. It was intimately linked to pressure to develop a new kind of strategic air arm, which followed from naval strategy and from the activities of wartime demagogues. As has been noted, England had never intended to send a large army to fight the German army. It was the Navy which was intended to make the greater contribution to England's war. The RNAS took the lead in extending air operations to German soil, with air-raids on German airship sheds and military targets. Indeed, the Admiralty had ordered heavy bombers from Handley Page as early as December 1914, although the first delivery of these 0/400s was not made until November 1916. The RNAS created a bomber wing in 1916, which did some bombing of Germany in 1916, but it was largely diverted to support of the Army in 1917.[17] Some naval aviators, however, wanted to bomb German targets systematically. Among them was a remarkable man named Noel Pemberton Billing.

Before the war Pemberton Billing had been an adventurer, soldier, actor, journalist, boxer, inventor and entrepreneur. His entrepreneurial activities ranged from horse-trading, ship-broking and property speculation, to the creation of a very famous aircraft firm. After a false start in 1908 he entered aviation with a vengeance in 1913. He bet Frederick Handley Page £500 that he could obtain his Royal Aero Club certificate within twenty-four hours of first sitting in an aeroplane. He managed to do it in just over four hours, though he almost killed himself in the process.[18] Nevertheless he went up again so that cine cameramen could record his feat. Pemberton Billing then started up a seaplane works at Woolston, near Southampton. This factory made 'PB' seaplanes, which 'PB' preferred to call 'supermarines', by analogy with 'submarines'. At the outbreak of war Pemberton Billing joined the RNAS, leaving it in late 1915 with the rank of Squadron Commander to enter politics. He lost a closely fought by-election in Mile End, and won East Hertfordshire in early 1916 despite the best efforts of the government. He ran a self-consciously modern and demagogic campaign using an aeroplane, films and phonographs.[19] His message was simple: reform the air services, escalate the air war and bomb civilians.[20] He had reached a ready audience because of the Zeppelin raids on London of 1915. Although the government-controlled press had turned against him, Pemberton Billing had the support of the powerful *Daily Mail*.

As a Member of Parliament he soon made two speeches which would have profound consequences. He took the lead in the campaign against the BE2c aeroplane, and by suggesting that airmen were being murdered by their own commanders by being sent up in them, forced the government to establish a judicial inquiry into the RFC.[21] This exonerated the RFC, but not the Royal Aircraft Factory. His dramatic intervention raised aeronautical politics to a new level, and Pemberton Billing became, with Horatio Bottomley, the leading demagogue of the war years. In the last year of the war he was the defendant in one of the most ludicrous but serious libel cases of the century.[22]

The summer and autumn of 1917 was the key period of agitation for a separate air force. Grotesquely, the death of some hundreds of civilians in German air-raids in the summer of 1917 transformed strategic debate, whereas deaths measured in hundreds of thousands on the Western Front had no such effect. The Northcliffe press again played a vital role in propaganda and agitation. It fell to Lord Smuts to report urgently to the government on the nation's air defences; but he went further in a second report of August 1917, to consider air strategy as a whole. He argued for a single unified air service, and for the bombing of Germany. The proposal was nearly shelved, but came back to life through the intercession of Admiral Mark Kerr of the Air Board, an air-power man, who provided an alarmist report of German air strength. This led to the passing, in November 1917, of the Air Force Act. This created a single Royal Air Force, uniting the RFC and RNAS, and a third service ministry, the Air Ministry.

Significantly enough, Lloyd George offered the job of Secretary of State for Air to Lord Northcliffe. Northcliffe contemptuously rejected it in an article in *The Times*, which he owned. The job went to his brother, Lord Rothermere, a newspaper proprietor in his own right and like his brother an air-power man. Rothermere was quickly replaced by William Weir, who in June 1918 created an Independent Air Force within the Royal Air Force. Weir was deeply committed to economic and economical warfare from the air: petrol was cheaper than cordite, he argued. By November 1918 the Independent Air Force was ready to bomb Berlin with new four-engined Handley Page bombers, and had already dropped more than twice the tonnage of bombs that the Germans had dropped on Britain in the whole war.[23]

Here was the shape of the things to come. An air force separate from the two traditional services, with an increasing emphasis on the bombing of civilians, a continuing association of aviation with right-wing politics and the right-wing popular press, and a deep concern on the part of the state with the economics of warfare.

2. Technology and Empire

Historians have agreed that English aviation was underdeveloped in the interwar years and have put forward many reasons for this. Yet we know that in the late 1930s German strength was overestimated and English strength underestimated, and that in 1940 the United Kingdom produced more aircraft than any other country in the world. This statistic is surely enough to dispel the image of industrial failure: to produce so many aircraft, and indeed such good aircraft, in 1940 implies that there was a fundamentally strong industry in 1935. Nevertheless historians emphasize weakness in the years prior to 1940, and particularly before 1935.

The charge is that the industry produced too few aircraft and that these aircraft, with the shining exception of the Schneider racers, were technically backward. Peter Fearon, the most careful student of the aircraft industry, has argued that:

> In the early postwar period the British aircraft industry was saved from virtual extinction by the Air Ministry which provided the means by which the manufacturers were able to keep their design teams together . . . Among the costs of the preservation of design competition was the survival of weak production units and the periodic poaching

> of business from the strong, often to the detriment of both. The Air Ministry was, of course, operating under considerable restraints such as financial hardship, public pacifism, and the temptations of Empire grandeur. Because of this many of its actions though questionable are understandable. The Ministry's cardinal error was to place so much emphasis on military aircraft at a time when there was no money and no demand for war machines. Thus the possibilities of producing a first-class civil airliner did not receive the attention they should have done.
>
> ... Without a viable internal market large sums of money coupled with far-sighted state direction might have halted Britain's aeronautical decline. The military aeroplanes produced for the Second World War showed that British designers were capable of producing all-metal monoplanes but had simply no call on their talents before rearmament. The budgetary history of the inter-war years, however, was that of reducing expenditure, rather than increasing it. Peace offered little incentive to military aircraft designers; the use of Imperial Airways as an instrument of Empire travel gave no challenge to civil aircraft designers. Hence Britain's poor position as an aeronautical power in 1935.[1]

These arguments for the causes of the failure of interwar aviation come from comparing the English industry not with that of other countries, but with an idealized model of technological and industrial development; as well as from a misleading analysis of the effects of empire, and an unwarranted assumption that defence expenditure was low.

This idealized model of technological and industrial development, which is very influential, overrates the power of modern technologies, overstresses civil technology, and sees large firms as the *sine qua non* of industrial modernity. Thus it is assumed that the economic and military power of modern technologies is dramatically greater than that of previous technologies. But in order to replace older technologies, substitutes need only be marginally better. Closely connected is a failure to consider the effects of alternative new technologies. In other words, the economic and military impact of new technologies is not properly measured. Thus despite the fact that mass aviation is a recent phenomenon – the man on the Clapham omnibus did not take to the air until the 1960s – and that the military value of air power has been called into question, it is assumed that England should have had a very big air force and very strong civil aviation in the interwar years. So strong is this kind of thinking that even critics of air power complain about the supposed lack of aeroplanes in the 1920s and early 1930s.

Another important feature of the idealized model is that modern technologies are thought to develop naturally from civil society, and that their usage is fundamentally civil. Even a militaristic historian like Correlli Barnett can say in criticism of the interwar aircraft industry that 'it was almost entirely an artificial creation by government in order to supply the needs of the Royal Air Force, rather than a spontaneous peacetime commercial growth to exploit a new international market'.[2] However, technologies do not develop autonomously: they are created with particular ends in mind. In the case of aircraft that end was, as we have seen, 'largely military rather than civil'. In England in 1934 the market for aircraft was divided as follows: Air Ministry £6 million; exports, mostly of military types, £1.5 million; home civil sales, £0.5 million.[3] Even in the United States the army and the navy accounted for at least 50 per cent of sales between 1927 and 1933, rising to at least two thirds in 1936. American aircraft exports rose from under 10 per cent of US production in the 1920s to over 40 per cent in the late 1930s largely because of sales of military types.[4] That aircraft were developed for war was an act of policy, backed up by public money. A world with no armed forces would have been a world with fewer and different aircraft in it.

Modern technologies are not only powerful and civil, they are also supposed to be produced by large firms on a large scale. Thus according to Barnett, the industry may be criticized because 'On the eve of major rearmament in 1936 . . . the British aircraft industry remained a cottage industry with obsolescent products; sleepy firms with facilities little more than experimental workshops employed hand-work methods and centred on their design departments.'[5] It is not difficult to reinforce this picture by cataloguing the collapse of firms after the First World War and highlighting the supposedly dreadful fact that some were forced to make car bodies and milk churns. There is, however, a fatal flaw in the argument: nowhere in the capitalist world were aircraft produced on the scale of motor-cars or electrical equipment or chemicals. There were no aeronautical equivalents of Ford, General

Electric or IG Farben: everywhere small and medium firms dominated aircraft production.

If failure in civil aviation was the key problem, historians have seen no salvation for the industry in orders from the RAF. As Barnett expresses it: 'The British aircraft industry as a whole had to be artificially kept alive by means of Air Ministry orders . . . and then only in tiny quantities because of the partial unilateral disarmament then being pursued by the British governments under the combined influence of moralizing internationalism and financial stringency.'[6] In fact, nearly all the major aircraft industries were kept alive by military orders, as we have noted. England, unique in the importance it attached to air power, had perhaps the largest aircraft industry in the world, and one which was deeply committed to technical development. Especially misleading is the charge that British governments engaged in 'partial unilateral disarmament'. The United Kingdom had the highest warlike expenditure in the world in absolute terms, and that of the Empire as a whole was even higher. The expenditure was probably higher in real terms than it had been in 1913 when a very visible potential enemy loomed over the North Sea.[7]

The end of the war, not surprisingly, saw huge cutbacks in armament production round the world, but this did not mean that defence expenditure stopped, even in defeated Germany. The new nations of central and eastern Europe created their own armed forces, and the victorious powers still had interests to maintain, notably imperial interests. Great Britain, France, Holland, Belgium, the United States, Japan, and even Portugal, Italy and Spain, were imperial nations. The greatest of these empires was the British Empire, now larger than it had ever been. In the interwar years the empires were at peace with each other, and there were good reasons for expecting there would be no new imperial war. But force was used to maintain empires, and in these campaigns aircraft became important. They were used by the English, the French, the Spanish, the Italians and the Americans in wars against insurgent populations. The Italians and the Japanese used them in wars of conquest.

At the end of the First World War the British Empire was the only one to have an independent air force and air ministry. This was not inevitable: in the 1920s, both the Army and the Navy wanted the RAF disbanded, not because they did not believe in air power, but because they did not believe in independent air power. They wanted to get their own air arms back. In its opposition to these takeover bids the RAF stressed the importance of independent strategic air power, which it argued made large armies and navies redundant. The RAF was fortunate in that the expanded British Empire gave it an opportunity to demonstrate this thesis. It proved itself to be a relatively cheap means of imperial control in sparsely populated new 'mandates' in the Middle East. In Mesopotamia (Iraq), Transjordan and Palestine, the RAF was put in charge of defence. The RAF later played an important role on the North-West Frontier.

It is too often assumed that commitments to Empire and to technology were antithetical to each other. The Empire is not part of the cruel real world, but instead is seen as a form of outdoor relief for aristocrats and out-of-date technologies. If it was outdoor relief, it greatly helped the development of English air power: commitment to the aeroplane was closely connected to commitment to Empire. Civil science and technology were also helped: by the late 1930s Imperial Civil Servants, often biologists, engineers and doctors, travelled to their posts with Imperial Airways, sent their despatches by the Empire Air Mail Service, and listened to the King Emperor on the Empire Service of the BBC. Technology and Empire were not in conflict with each other: they were symbiotically linked.

Despite the importance of its imperial role, the RAF was not committed to Empire at the expense of the European theatre. The great concern expressed at the expansion of the French air force in the 1920s indicated the extent to which it was already believed that air power would be decisive in a future European war. The scare led to expansion of the RAF as a European bomber force. By the mid-1930s the RAF, secure in its independence, was destined to become England's principal weapon against Germany, and the vast majority of its modern aircraft were deployed in England. As will be discussed in the following chapter, this was a reflection of England's commitment to cheap, technological war.

The Industrial Basis of Air Power

The idea that the Air Ministry was short of money for the purchase of aircraft, and that somehow the amount of money available fell in the interwar years, bears little relationship to reality. Although the RAF was the smallest of the services in terms of total expenditure until 1939, it spent a particularly high proportion of its resources on new equipment. And if we look at the expenditure of each of the three services on armaments and warlike stores, we find that the Air Ministry took a disproportionate share of expenditure. In 1924–5 the figures were Navy £13 million; RAF £6.9 million; Army £2.6 million. By 1932–3, however, the figures were Navy £10.3 million, RAF £8.7 million; Army £1.8 million. Thus, RAF procurement expenditure *increased* dramatically between 1924 and 1932, in which year it was taking about 45 per cent of armed service procurement expenditure. As will be discussed further below, the RAF took an even greater share of the resources devoted to defence research and development (R&D). The big picture we should have in mind, then, is of a *growing* industry.

Immediately after the war, of course, expenditure on aircraft was cut back drastically and many wartime producers went out of business. The number of ordinary members of the Society of British Aircraft Constructors (SBAC), the trade association established in 1916, fell to thirty-five, and within a few years had halved.[8] New export markets and growth in civil aviation could not make up for the huge cut-back. Nevertheless, by the early 1920s the industry was on an even keel and about to expand again.

All the major armourers decided to stay in aircraft production. Armstrong-Whitworth set up a separate aircraft subsidiary, took over the Coventry-based Siddeley Deasy company (largely because it wanted the Puma engine), and concentrated airframe production in Coventry also. The airframe firm was named the Sir W. G. Armstrong-Whitworth Aircraft Company, and the engine company the Armstrong Siddeley Motor Company. In 1926, as the parent armament firm Armstrong-Whitworth went into crisis, Sir John Siddeley bought up the two firms. Vickers, which would merge with Armstrong-Whitworth in 1927, retained its interest in aircraft and bought a shareholding in S. E. Saunders; in 1928 it bought Supermarine. Beardmore, who had made and designed aircraft and engines, did not last long as producers after the war, but re-entered the industry in 1924–9 to build a number of seaplanes and a huge monoplane landplane for the Air Ministry using the German stressed-skin Rohrbach method. Coventry Ordnance Works was taken over in the merger which created English Electric, and aircraft production was continued for a while in Preston.

The free-standing aircraft firms had a harder time. The Sopwith Aviation Company was liquidated and reformed as Hawker Engineering; A. V. Roe was taken over by Crossley Engineering to make car bodies, but also continued to make aircraft. Sometimes firms were lost but design teams kept together. Airco, the largest wartime producer, was taken over by the small-arms, motor-cycle and car (Daimler) firm BSA for its plant, but it spawned two independent aircraft firms, de Havilland and Gloster Aircraft. The Handley Page company tried car assembly and lost a lot of money. It also sent export missions all round the world, incurring a loss of over £250,000 by the end of 1920. Handley Page Transport, established in 1919, made losses of over £100,000. Handley Page was also heavily involved financially in the Aircraft Disposal Company, which was set up in 1920 to buy from the Ministry of Munitions the massive amounts of war-surplus equipment. Handley Page's financial involvement in ADC was very complex, but income from ADC sales, and from the sale of his air transport firm to Imperial Airways in 1924, kept Handley Page going.

The Bristol Company, under strong Air Ministry pressure, took over a highly successful engine design team led by Roy Fedden. Fedden had been with the Bristol car firm Brazil Straker, who produced Rolls-Royce aero-engines during the war, and he went on to design his own. Bristol engines were very successful in the 1920s and 1930s: not only were many exported but foreign firms acquired licences (including the mighty French company Gnome et Rhône) which brought in tens of millions of pounds. By 1930 Bristol provided 'the principal engine of nearly half the world's airlines and more than half the air forces'.[9] Of the many firms which made and designed aero-engines during the war, only two others stayed on as significant forces in the industry: Rolls-Royce and Napier.

By the mid-1920s the shake-out was over. Between 1924 and 1930 the output, employment and exports of the aircraft industry had doubled and thereafter were broadly static. The firms supplying the Air Ministry were fairly secure in the knowledge that the Ministry would not let them go out of business: indeed, no major firm left aircraft or engine production between the mid-1920s and the 1950s. There were no new major entrants to aircraft or engine design until the end of the Second World War.

1. The Air Ministry 'Ring', 1934

	Firm	*Location*	*Products*
1	Armstrong Siddeley*	Coventry	engines
2	Armstrong-Whitworth*	Coventry	airframes
3	Blackburn	Yorkshire	airframes
4	Boulton Paul	Norwich	airframes
5	Bristol	Bristol	airframes and engines
6	De Havilland	London	airframes and engines
7	Fairey	London	airframes
8	Gloster**	Gloucestershire	airframes
9	Hawker**	London	airframes
10	Napier	London	engines
11	Handley Page	London	airframes
12	Avro*	Manchester	airframes
13	Rolls-Royce	Derby	engines
14	Saunders Roe	Isle of Wight	airframes
15	Short Bros	Kent	airframes
16	Supermarine***	Southampton	airframes
17	Vickers***	London	airframes
18	Westland	Yeovil	airframes

** / ** / *** indicate common ownership.*

The pre-rearmament aircraft firms were not as small or as poor as is sometimes implied. The larger firms – Hawker, the Siddeley firms and Fairey – were very profitable companies. Fairey and Hawker were making over £100,000 per annum. Others, for example Handley Page, had sales less than this in some years in the early 1930s.[10] Most firms were reasonably large: in 1935 the eleven largest airframe makers (including the components of Hawker Siddeley) were all employing between 1,000 and 2,000 workers. The industry was also more financially concentrated than the picture of a cottage industry implies. In 1928 Sir John Siddeley, who already had Armstrong-Whitworth and Armstrong Siddeley, bought A. V. Roe of Manchester. Siddeley thus controlled a large proportion of the aircraft industry in the north of England, the exceptions being Blackburn and Rolls-Royce. In 1935 there was an important merger in the industry which brought together Hawker (who had taken over Gloster in 1934), with the Siddeley firms, to form Hawker Siddeley, with Sir John Siddeley as Managing Director. Hawker Siddeley thus had airframe plants near London (Kingston upon Thames – Hawker); Coventry (Armstrong-Whitworth); Gloucestershire (Gloster); and Manchester (Avro), as well as an engine plant in Coventry (Armstrong Siddeley): it employed over 13,000 workers, putting it in the top thirty British manufacturing employers. Vickers, the fourth largest manufacturing employer in Britain, employed about 3,500 on aircraft production in November 1935.[11]

Running through the criticisms of the aircraft industry

in the interwar years is the implication that other countries' aircraft industries were stronger. International comparisons are very difficult but they should at least be attempted. Unfortunately, no proper comparative statistics of aircraft industries in the 1920s and 1930s exist. Tallies of total numbers of aircraft produced disguise wide variations in the types of aircraft, and the value of output might hide very different costs of production. Table 2, showing the numbers of workers employed in aircraft industries, should also be approached with caution, since we might expect the productivity of labour to vary between countries and from year to year. But we may conclude from Table 2 that the English industry was at least as large as any other into the early 1930s.

There is another index which may be used to show the strength of the aircraft industry. In the mid-1930s the only net exporters of aircraft were Britain, France, Germany, the United States and Italy. Until the mid-1930s Britain was probably the largest exporter of aircraft of them all. Aeronautical exports need to be put into the context of English arms exports in the interwar years. In the late 1920s and early 1930s Britain was the largest exporter of armaments in the world, having something like 20–30 per cent of this trade, worth around £6 million. About £2 million of this was military aircraft, engines and spares.[12] Such an impression of strength is corroborated by a claim in *The Aeroplane* in 1936 that Britain had been in aggregate the largest exporter of aircraft in the world.[13]

2. Estimates of Employment in Aircraft Industries, 1924–39 (thousands)

	Germany	*UK*	*France*	*USA*
1924	12	13		
1929			18	19
1930	21	20		
1932	4			
1933	12			10
1934	46	24	22	
1935	84	35	24	
1936	188	60	32	
1937	229		33	
1938	293	120	47	
1939	140	110	64	

The figures are approximate, and it is unclear how comparable they are.
Sources: Germany: E. L. Homze, *Arming the Luftwaffe: The Reich Air Ministry and the German Aircraft Industry, 1919–1939* (Nebraska, 1976), pp. 37, 184. UK: Peter Fearon, 'Aircraft Manufacturing', in D. H. Aldcroft and N. K. Buxton (eds.), *British Industry Betweeen the Wars* (London, 1979), p. 216. France: Emmanuel Chadeau, *L'Industrie aéronautique en France, 1900–1950: de Blériot à Dassault* (Paris, 1987), p. 441. USA: J. B. Rae, *Climb to Greatness* (Cambridge, Mass., 1968), p. 83.

The Air Ministry was strongly supportive of the efforts of private firms. The case of the mission to Japan in the early 1920s shows just how far encouragement could go. The Imperial Japanese Navy was very keen to develop naval aviation and asked England, the leading naval aviation power, to send an official mission to train pilots and to supply aircraft. The Admiralty was against this, but the Air Ministry instead sent an 'unofficial' mission, ostensibly concerned with civil aviation. This 1921 mission comprised nineteen officers as well as design staff, and involved the sale to Japan of 113 aircraft, mostly of post-war manufacture. It was led by a noted aviator, Colonel the Master of Sempill. Through the remainder of the 1920s Sempill would act as a salesman for aircraft firms, and was an adviser to the Greek Naval Air Service. It was only many years after his death that it was publicly revealed that he had been spying for the Japanese until 1941.

Unfortunately we have no systematic knowledge of where aircraft went, but we do have some details. There was an Avro mission to the Spanish Navy in the 1920s; Vickers also operated in Spain, where Vildebeests were made. Armstrong-Whitworth sold aeroplanes to Romania. Fairey established a plant in Belgium in 1931 to manufacture military aircraft based on the Fairey Fox and Firefly, and in the early 1930s sold some aircraft to the Russians, as well as to Argentina, Brazil and Peru. The Blackburn company acted as managers for the Greek government's aircraft factory and sold aircraft to the Portuguese Navy. Hawker sold to Estonia, Yugoslavia, Japan, Portugal and Iraq, and granted licences to the Danish and Swedish governments. As far as civil aviation is concerned, de

Havilland established plants in Australia and then Canada, and in the 1920s Handley Page airliners were licensed to a Belgian company. As we shall see, the sale of arms abroad was to become a controversial issue in the early 1930s, and aircraft manufacturers came in for their share of criticism.

Air Ministry Ordering Policy 1920–35

The intention of the Air Ministry in establishing a 'ring' of 'approved firms' was above all to sustain a range of design units, and to stimulate technical progress by having a number of firms competing in designs of aircraft of every given type. The RAF used many different types of aircraft and its forces were continually re-equipped. To give some examples of the production of each firm: Gloster produced Gauntlets and Gladiators; Vickers produced Valettas and Vildebeests; Hawker produced Harts and Hinds; Westland produced Wapitis; Handley Page produced Hainadis and Heyfords. On the engine side Rolls-Royce produced Eagles and Kestrels; Armstrong Siddeley, Pumas and Tigers; Bristol both Jupiters and Mercuries; Napier made Lions, Rapiers and Daggers. These are just examples of aircraft and engines which went into production: many more prototypes were built.

The standard procedure for ordering new aircraft in this period was as follows. A specification, drawn up by the RAF and Air Ministry technicians, would be issued to 'approved firms'. These firms would then submit designs and tenders for prototypes; the Air Ministry would then place contracts for a number of these; from the prototypes one aircraft, or perhaps more, would be chosen for production. The production order was usually given to the designing firm, but in some cases production was itself put out to tender, although the designing firm always got some production orders. The firms did not like this at all: they wanted production contracts to go entirely to the designing firm, which would if necessary arrange its own subcontracting. On the whole orders were too small to warrant spreading construction over more than one firm, but certain large orders were spread to keep firms in work, and to prevent firms expanding beyond a viable size. Two notable examples were orders for the Armstrong-Whitworth Siskin and the Hawker Hart. Four hundred and eighty-five Siskins of various types were built, of which 348 were Siskin IIIAs; of these 252 were built by Blackburn, Bristol, Gloster and Vickers.[14] A total of 1,042 Hawker Harts in different variants were built, of which Gloster built 72, Armstrong-Whitworth 450 and Vickers 226.[15]

The private manufacturers had a second complaint against the Air Ministry. They wanted almost complete freedom from the Ministry in matters of design as well as production. To justify this argument they made much of their 'private ventures' (a term long used in the arms industry to denote design and development projects done without reference to the procurer's specifications and financed by the firm – a situation so rare that a special term is needed). In the ten years 1924 to 1934, claimed the

SBAC, one in three 'private ventures' were accepted for service by the RAF, compared to one in six specification types. The implication was that letting firms design as they pleased was the best policy. A number of points may be made: first, private ventures were rare, which is why they were given a special name. Secondly, while a design might start as a private venture, the building of a prototype as a private venture was even rarer, and the private financing of production aircraft was almost unheard of. But the key point is that the Air Ministry strongly favoured private design and financed a great deal of it: the firms were arguing for state finance with no state control.

The Air Ministry, with the exception of the 'socialist' airship project launched by the Labour government of 1924, did not undertake design or production, unlike the War Office and the Admiralty. There was a case, however, for a return to the situation where a Royal Aircraft Factory designed aircraft and engines and undertook limited manufacture; or indeed, for the nationalization of the entire industry. In the early and mid-1930s, the left and influential elements in the centre of English politics called for the nationalization of the industry, as part of a wholesale nationalization of the arms industry. For perhaps the majority the purpose of nationalization was to control the excesses of the armourers in order to prevent war, but for some it was a means of improving the efficiency of the industry. There was an important public forum for the discussion of these issues in the mid-1930s, the Royal Commission on the Private Manufacture of and Trading in Arms. This little-known Royal Commission was appointed in February 1935 in response to allegations that the major private armourers fomented war scares and indulged in bribery to secure contracts from foreign powers. During 1935 there was great interest in the public hearings but by 1936, when the Commission reported, this had declined. Because the work of the Royal Commission coincided with the beginnings of rearmament, a considerable proportion of its deliberations were concerned with how rearmament could best be organized. In these discussions the aircraft industry had a place commensurate with its increasing importance in defence.

The case for the nationalization of the aircraft industry on efficiency grounds was put by Ronald McKinnon Wood, a socialist aeronautical engineer who had worked at Farnborough between 1914 and 1934. He argued that the new aircraft 'bearing the name of some aircraft company' was 'by no means the product of the private industry; it is the product in the proportion 50–50 of state research and private enterprise in design'.[16] Secondly, he argued that the number of design units in existence was too large: individual design units were too small to be efficient and there was duplication of effort. He had found that inter-firm technical secrecy was a problem:

> I often found myself in the difficult position – acting as one does in the Government research service to a very large extent, as a free consulting engineer to the aeroplane designer – in the difficulty that I was unable to bring these . . . ideas together, in the interests of fair

> competition between rivals who were competing in business to a common specification.[17]

While he was not against competition as such, he believed that inter-firm secrecy at least delayed the introduction of new methods. McKinnon Wood's answer to these problems was to nationalize the industry, which would be run by a Corps of Aircraft Constructors, by analogy with the Admiralty's Corps of Naval Constructors.

The opposition to the idea of a nationalized aircraft industry, or even a government aircraft factory, was vehement. Major R. H. Mayo, the technical adviser to Imperial Airways (and inventor of the Mayo Composite aircraft), argued that 'in the present state of the art, and for some years to come, competition in the basic design is of vital importance in both civil and military aviation'; private enterprise was essential because it led to such competition, 'with no overriding design authority to cause stereotyping of ideas'. In addition, he argued that 'aircraft design is still in such a state of flux that no government institution could possibly keep pace with the requirements',[18] the exception being, one assumes, the Royal Air Force! The SBAC argued that 'any aeroplane which is submitted for testing by the Royal Air Force is wholly the product of the designing firm': Air Ministry specifications held the industry back; Ministry design would be even worse.

The RAF, the Air Ministry and the government agreed. Sir Hugh Dowding, at that time responsible for research and development, said the Air Ministry was definitely against even the partial construction of an airframe or engine in a government factory. Lord Weir, now industrial adviser to the Air Minister, Lord Swinton, accepted that new designs were approximately equally the work of the state and the industry, but saw private, competitive design as essential:

> I know of many industries where I would consider [full state] control necessary and valuable, but in Air, which is still developing its scientific possibilities, and which demands engagement of the imagination and enterprise of the individual, I am frankly rather scared at the possible dangers of centralized direction.[19]

Although the Royal Commission rejected the case for the abolition of the private manufacture of arms, the rejection was qualified by recommendations of greater state control over rearmament. Indeed, it recommended that the Air Ministry should establish a factory to act as a technical leader in design and development and as a training centre for techniques of mass production. The government rejected the recommendation, restating the case for private design in colourful terms:

> As regards aircraft, the state of progress of the industry is a fundamental reason against manufacture of machines and engines in government factories. Such manufacture would inevitably lead to premature standardization of types in an industry of which the principal characteristic at present, and probably for a considerable time to come

> is rapid development and improvement sometimes of an almost revolutionary character. The strongest possible competition in design – inspired by the best brains working under conditions most favourable to and provocative of invention and progress – is essential to the maintenance of the highest levels of efficiency.[20]

It was not until the late 1930s, and especially during the war, that the policy of relying exclusively on private firms for design was reconsidered. Meanwhile the conditions held to be 'most favourable to and provocative of invention and progress' were very firmly private enterprise. There was much to commend the policy. It was difficult to predict which design team would produce the best aircraft and therefore having many design teams might help produce a winner. It is perhaps just as well that firms like Armstrong-Whitworth, Fairey and Gloster, all very successful in the 1920s, did not come to monopolize aircraft production in the 1930s, at least if one is to judge from their later records. Equally, it is fortunate that a small flying-boat maker like Supermarine did not go out of business, or a firm like Avro, which made trainers.

Civil Aviation in the Interwar Years

The Air Ministry did not control civil aviation in the way it controlled the RAF. There was a general presumption that civil aviation was a matter for the private sector, although subsidies were granted from the early 1920s. Civil aviation got off the ground as soon as restrictions on civil flying were lifted in 1919. The first company to inaugurate international services, Aircraft Transport and Travel, was controlled by George Holt Thomas. It was soon joined by Handley Page and Instone Airlines. These companies very quickly stopped flying and it was not until the Air Ministry granted them subsidies that civil transport started again. In 1924 the major airlines were merged to form Imperial Airways: this was a successor to the Holt Thomas firm, the Supermarine airline (formed in 1923), and the Handley Page line. The government subsidized the private firm with a total of £1m over ten years; private investors were required to put up the same amount. Imperial Airways, however, received a smaller subsidy than did the major Continental airlines.

Imperial Airways had a bad press. It was smaller than the Continental airlines and its equipment was, and is, regarded as out of date. Two famous aircraft sum up this image: the HP42s of the early 1930s, and the Short Empire flying boats of the late 1930s. The ungainly and slow Handley Page HP42s were large four-engined biplanes, which were used on both European and Imperial Airways services; they were introduced in 1931 and Imperial Airways was operating these quaintly backward aircraft into the late 1930s. The Short flying boats, introduced in the late 1930s, though often remembered with nostalgia, have been seen by many as a classic example of imperial delusions triumphing over commercial common sense and leading English aviation up a blind alley.

But these were not the only large aircraft operated by Imperial Airways in the 1930s. In the early years they were also operating large four-engined monoplanes, the Armstrong-Whitworth Atalanta. Similarly, in the late 1930s, four-engined stressed-skin Armstrong-Whitworth Ensigns were used. But in any case, flying boats were not a dead end: many countries used them, not least the United States. Furthermore the Americans used them for imperial purposes: it is no accident that the main operator was named Pan American (which sounds better, for some reason, than Pan German or Imperial). Nevertheless, given the slowness of the introduction of Ensigns into the European service, the Tory MP, aviator and engineer, W. Robert Perkins could with justice say that: 'Imperial Airways services in Europe are the laughing stock of the world . . . when I am sitting in some distant aerodrome in Europe in the summer and a kind of Heath Robinson machine descends from the skies and everyone begins to laugh, I feel thoroughly ashamed.'[21] Unfortunately for Imperial Airways, Heath Robinson aeroplanes (in Europe) were not its only problem. It was accused of paying over-large dividends on the back of state subsidies and of victimizing the leadership of the British Airline Pilots Association. The government appointed a commission of enquiry which upheld many of the charges against the airline, and before the beginning of the war it was nationalized. The government had acted on what had become a national scandal. By this time new aircraft had been introduced, including the beautiful wooden, stressed-skin de Havilland four-engined airliner. De Havilland were also designing a twin-engined metal airliner, production of which was cut short by the war. In 1938 both Fairey and Shorts started design work on four-engined metal airliners, both financed by the Air Ministry. Neither came to fruition because of the war.

The Technical Development of Aviation

Historians who have argued that the English industry became increasingly backward technologically by the mid-1930s have usually relied on very limited and impressionistic evidence, for example, that England relied on biplanes for longer than other nations, and invested in flying boats rather than landplanes. We have dealt briefly with the flying-boat issue, but there remains the general question of the relative technical quality of English aircraft. Unfortunately, we have no large-scale comparative study of the performance of aircraft in the interwar years. Perhaps this is not surprising, since comparing the performance of aircraft is very difficult. The aeroplane, military and civil, is a particularly subtle and multi-faceted machine which is difficult to reduce to numerical indices of performance. Indeed, many of the widely used indices, like speed, range or weight, do not capture the complexities of aircraft. Record-breaking can be an especially misleading indicator since the real skill of the designer consisted not in maximizing speed, height or range, but rather in optimizing particular combinations for particular uses. To make the issue even more complex, designers had to concern themselves with ranges of speeds, loads and heights. All aircraft have to take off and land, and therefore have to operate at low speeds and low altitudes, however high and however fast they eventually travel; they also have to fly laden and unladen.

Appearance can be deceptive too. Technological change in the 1920s has been underestimated because aircraft of 1930 looked like aircraft of 1918. And yet the 1920s saw a change in materials and methods of construction: by the mid-1920s aircraft tended to be made of steel rather than wood; some were clad in fabric, others in wood or metal. More important still was the changing shape of wings and the consequent change in their aerodynamic qualities. But perhaps the most important changes of all came in engines. A typical military aero-engine of 1935 had a horsepower in the range of 500–900, while the largest engines in use at the end of the Great War produced about 250 horsepower. The newer engines were much more reliable (a critical factor in aviation) and lighter for their power output. This was made possible by higher precision engineering, better materials and better fuels.

Another example of the deceptiveness of appearance concerns the transition from biplane to monoplane. It is wrong to assume that monoplanes had a decisive edge; a whole range of factors was involved in improving performance, strength, weight and landing speed, as well as top speed. For a long period the trade-off was a fine one. Biplanes were, in many functions, dominant into the mid-1930s because they could be made lighter than monoplanes for a given wing area; they also had lower landing speeds (hence the continued use of biplanes on aircraft-carriers after they had been phased out on land). But in certain cases the trade-off worked decisively in favour of monoplanes, notably in that of high-speed racing planes. From the mid-1920s world speed records were held by monoplanes. As is well known, an English monoplane racer won the world speed record with a speed of more than 400 miles per hour in 1931. This aeroplane provides the most clichéd image in the history of English aviation. The racer won the Schneider trophy and is widely regarded as the one aircraft of the interwar years that bucked the trend of backwardness in English aeronautical technology. This is not all. Since it was designed by R. J. Mitchell at Supermarine and used a Rolls-Royce engine, it is made to appear as an early version of the Spitfire. It was not: it was a highly specialized aeroplane, designed to fly very fast over a short distance at sea level, unlike the Spitfire. It did not need to be manoeuvrable, or to have a high climb rate, or operate at high altitude; its engine did not need to be particularly reliable, or to have a long life between services, or be fuel efficient, and it was none of these things. But perhaps the most obvious difference between the racer and the Spitfire gives the best indication of the complexities of analysing aeronautical progress: the fact that the racer was a seaplane. Although it seems strange, given the additional drag caused by the floats, seaplanes could have higher maximum speeds than landplanes. This was because seaplanes could land at much higher speeds than landplanes. Having a high landing speed made it easier to reach high speeds since making a high-speed wing was not difficult in itself; the difficulty lay in making a wing which could be used for a wide range of speeds.[22] Indeed, landplanes did not achieve the world speed record until the late 1930s; in the early 1930s landplane speed records were at least 100 miles per hour less than seaplane records.

The Schneider racer illustrates well how two indices, speed and structure, are not enough to describe an aeroplane. If we choose our indices carefully we can make aircraft seem modern or out of date. To take examples from the late 1930s and early 1940s: the Vickers Wellington had a geodetic fabric-covered structure rather than the aluminium-alloy sheet skin typical of modern aircraft of the late 1930s. The Hawker Hurricane, which was almost as effective as the Spitfire and much more economical to manufacture, was fabric-covered. The de Havilland Mosquito was made of wood! No one calls these aircraft out of date, but that is because they belong to the heroic period of the Second World War, and because they were very successful aircraft, especially the Mosquito.

Research 1920–35

Early aircraft may have looked like contraptions, but they were very complex machines, operating in complex and variable environments. It is little wonder then that governments everywhere saw the need for scientific research in aviation. In England, as has been noted, aeronautical research was firmly established before the First World

War. In the interwar years it was stronger than before the war, and perhaps stronger than during the war itself. The RAF and the Air Ministry prided themselves on their support of research and technological development. In the 1920s and early 1930s the Air Ministry's R & D spending represented more than 20 per cent of total expenditure on aircraft and equipment. The Air Ministry was easily the largest R & D spending institution in Britain. In the mid-1920s it was spending £1.34 million on R & D, compared with £0.98 million by the Admiralty, and £0.49 million by the War Office. The largely civil Department of Scientific and Industrial Research (DSIR), which has received quite disproportionate attention from historians, was spending a mere £0.38 million.[23] For the mid-1930s we can make a comparison with industrial R & D spending. In 1935–6 the Air Ministry spent £1.25 million on R & D, while industry spent at least £2.7 million (the figure is an underestimate). ICI, the largest industrial R & D performer, spent £0.59 million. Thus aeronautical development was a vitally important component of the national R & D effort, even before rearmament. Most of the Ministry's R & D expenditure financed the design and development of new types by and in the private firms. Research was concentrated at the former Royal Aircraft Factory, renamed the Royal Aircraft Establishment (RAE), and at the National Physical Laboratory which now came under the Department of Scientific and Industrial Research.

Aeronautical research was a high-status activity. Two interwar holders of the prestigious post of Director of the National Physical Laboratory (NPL) were engineers closely

1. 'Wonders of Science' by Will Dyson, 1914–1915: the Germans bring together modern science and primitive barbarism, a common propaganda theme. Dyson, who was Australian, became an official war artist.

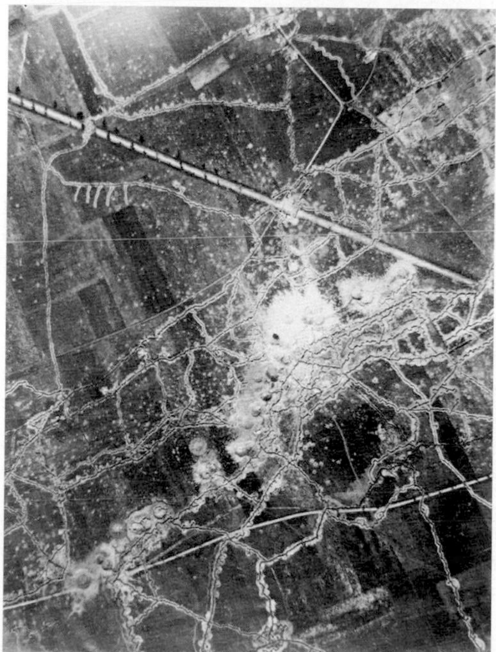

2. (*opposite*) Aerial photograph of German infantry on the Marne, 1914–1918. Taking aerial photographs was one of the main roles of the Royal Flying Corps.

3. (*above*) Aerial photograph of Ypres, 1916. The damage was done by artillery.

4. (*left*) Trenches near Loos, 1917. Note the cratering around no-man's land.

5. Bomb damage caused by the Independent Air Force, Germany, 1918. The ending of the war cut short the campaign by the new Royal Air Force and its Independent Air Force to bomb Germany.

6. Supermarine S6 racer being prepared for the Schneider Trophy contest, 1929. R. J. Mitchell is on the right. He also designed the winning aircraft for the previous (1927) and subsequent (1931) races.

7. Imperial Airways HP42, a photograph used by Le Corbusier in his book *Aircraft* (1935) makes this ungainly aeroplane look chic.

8. *Aircraftman, 1942* by Sir William Rothenstein. Unlike the officer in illustration 9, this 'erk' is anonymous.

9. *Flying Officer J. H. Laughlin MBE* by Sir William Rothenstein. Rothenstein was an official war artist for the RAF.

10. *Target area: Whitley bombers over Berlin*, 1940 by Paul Nash. Watercolour derived from photographs, one of the last images Nash made for the Air Ministry, who preferred more traditional images, for examples see illustrations 8 and 9.

connected to aeronautical research. Henry Tizard, the Oxford chemist who had worked on aeronautics in the war, and was an expert on aviation fuels, became Secretary of the Department of Scientific and Industrial Research and Rector of Imperial College. From 1933 he was also Chairman of the Aeronautical Research Committee (successor to the ACA); during the Second World War he was a member of the Air Council. University aeronautical research was highly concentrated in elite institutions. A national school of aeronautical engineering under Bertram Hopkinson, the Cambridge professor of engineering, had been planned but the scheme was aborted on Hopkinson's death in an air crash in 1918. Instead, Cambridge and Imperial College, London, became the main centres of research and education. In Cambridge a chair was endowed which was first held by Bennett Melville Jones, between 1919 and 1952! Jones was a believer in the scientist pilot, and airborne investigations were regularly carried out in conjunction with the University Air Squadron, which was established in 1927. In 1935 Sir John Siddeley gave £10,000 for aeronautical research to Cambridge, despite angry protests by Cambridge socialists. W. S. Farren (later Superintendent of the RAE) was a consultant to Armstrong-Whitworth, part of the Siddeley empire. At Imperial College, the Royal Naval Air Service had established a laboratory during the war under H. E. Wimperis (who became the first Director of Research at the Air Ministry in 1924), and this laboratory continued to be funded by the Air Ministry. The notorious arms dealer Sir Basil Zaharoff endowed a chair in aviation at

Imperial College: in true 'merchant of death' style Zaharoff had already endowed chairs in Paris and St Petersburg. The first Zaharoff Professor was the former head of the NPL, Sir Richard Glazebrook. In 1920 Leonard Bairstow, who had headed the NPL's Aerodynamics department between 1909 and 1917, became Professor of Aerodynamics, and succeeded to the Zaharoff Chair in 1923, heading the Department of Aeronautics at Imperial College until 1945.

The results of aeronautical research were impressive. Theory and experiment led to the specification of standard wing shapes with well understood aerodynamic properties, and to new fuels, materials and constructional techniques. As has been noted, the extent of the contribution of state research was an issue over which there had been controversy from well before the First World War, but it was clearly important. In the interwar years there were great advances in aerodynamic theory drawing on the work of Ludwig Prandtl of the University of Goettingen, the principal centre of German aerodynamics. Before and during the First World War Prandtl developed a complete mathematical theory of lift and drag which was introduced to the English-speaking world by the RAE. Using Prandtl's work and new experimental results, B. M. Jones calculated the minimum drag of a wing. This was much lower than was previously thought and alerted designers to the possibilities of both crude and detailed streamlining. This theoretical computation of what was possible may be compared with that made in the early nineteenth century concerning the maximum possible efficiency of steam engines, which showed engineers how much energy was being wasted. Theory could also, and just as importantly, tell engineers what was not possible. Thus in the late 1920s, a young RAF officer, Frank Whittle, who studied aeronautics at Cambridge, concluded that piston engines and propellers could not be used for high-speed high-altitude flight. This led him to consider gas-turbine jet engines instead.

What were the results of the state's support of the aircraft industry in the interwar years? Consideration of the re-armament effort after 1935 is left to a subsequent chapter, but it is nevertheless useful to have some indication of England's aeronautical position in 1939–40. Malcolm Smith suggests that the strengths of the RAF and the *Luftwaffe* on 1 September 1939 were about equal in terms of numbers of bombers and interceptor fighters.[24] In 1940 the United Kingdom was the largest aircraft producer in the world, making 50 per cent more than the Germans. In terms of the quality of aircraft, comparisons are even more unreliable. But as far as fighters are concerned the consensus is that the best on each side were about equal. Bombers did not fight each other, so comparisons are more difficult. Some authorities stress the similarities between the basic type of German and English bombers, others suggest that the German aeroplanes were marginally better. Perhaps the safest, simplest conclusion one can come to is that there is no failure of the British aircraft industry in the interwar years which needs to be explained.

3. Going Up for Air

Despite the increasing quantity of revisionist historiography which seeks to portray Neville Chamberlain as a rational strategist, other images of the interwar years continue to dominate political and popular attitudes. Thus, speaking at the Conservative Party rally in October 1989, Mrs Thatcher, adding years to her age, noted that: 'Some of us remember all too well what happened in the 1920s and 1930s when we allowed our hopes for a peaceful world to outrun our judgements on the need for defence. The world paid a terrible price'.[1]

According to 'Cato', writing in 1940, Baldwin's premiership in the 1920s had five notable features: the return to Gold, the General Strike, an 'eloquent debate' on the Prayer Book, the decline of agriculture, and the 'reduction of British air power to fifth in world rank'.[2] Baldwin and MacDonald 'took over a great empire, supreme in arms and secure in liberty' which by the late 1930s was 'on the edge of national annihilation', measured by unemployment, workers leaving the land, an air force now ranked sixth, and an army without weapons.[3] MacDonald, Baldwin and the rest were seen as bloodless, complacent and lazy: what a contrast to the men of action, Churchill and the macho Welsh Wizard, Lloyd George, even in his dotage. Cato's image, too, is still important, though the Prayer

Book, the Empire and agriculture are now commonly left out. In other ways, the charge sheet has been lengthened to include a wider range of people and new crimes. The whole political, social and intellectual elite is seen not only as pathetically idealistic about the world, but also as anti-scientific, anti-technological and anti-industrial. We are invited to see interwar culture, in the widest sense, as the pastel-coloured preciousness of Bloomsbury, and as a yearning for the rural. Even communist intellectuals are seen as literary types. We are asked to accept, by implication, a picture of interwar England which was more liberal, internationalist and anti-militarist than it had been in the Edwardian years.

One would not guess from this picture that the British Empire was at the height of its size, that defence expenditure in the 1920s was higher than it had ever been in peacetime, and higher than any other nation. Or that public schoolboys and some university students were now drilled in Officers' Training Corps, an Edwardian innovation. Imperialism as an ideology was more widespread and uncontroversial than it had ever been: many schoolchildren celebrated Empire Day from 1904, with from 1916 greater official endorsement. Actions are just as important as ideas and capacities: if the British Empire appeased Nazi Germany in the late 1930s, it did not appease the Soviet Union or colonial opposition. Although the government did not want war in 1939, it introduced conscription in *peacetime* for the first time, and created a Ministry of Supply before war was declared. England went to war in September 1939 believing that its cities would suffer massive casualties from bombing. If England went to war innocently in 1914, it did not do so in 1939.

If we focus on the social, political and ideological aspects of interwar aviation, it is especially clear that the received view needs revising. English enthusiasm for aeroplanes and aeronautical rearmament often went along with support for Empire and the European dictators. This should not be surprising given that the most enthusiastic supporters of aviation before and during the Great War had been men of the right. Nevertheless, it is surprising because so much of the literature on aviation and on defence policy in the interwar years stresses the liberal antipathy to armaments, and bombing aeroplanes especially, as characteristic of attitudes as a whole. We need to examine these liberal attitudes, but we also need to recognize that opposition to armaments was a minority activity, blown up out of all proportion by later detractors and some supporters. It is important to remember, too, that in interwar England, the monarchy, the state, the Empire and the armed services were largely immune from criticism in the important communications media: the cinema, the radio and most of the newspapers.

Liberals, the Left and Aviation

In the interwar years, and particularly in the early 1930s, there was an upsurge in opposition to war. In the late 1920s and early 1930s there was a spate of war memoirs and books on the horrors of war which revealed the continuing strength of a liberal internationalist position on world affairs. However, the interwar anti-war movement differed in some interesting respects from its classic liberal antecedents. In the nineteenth century, liberals had argued that free trade led to peace; states, especially aristocratic states, caused war. Furthermore, to privatize armaments production was to take out of the hands of the warmongering aristocracy the means to make war. Related was their argument that technical advance, best pursued by private individuals, would produce technology which would be both international and internationalizing, and thus peace-creating. Modern technology, if applied to warfare, would make war unthinkable because of its destructiveness. In the interwar years, by contrast, the feeling developed that the First World War had in part been caused by the large private manufacturers of armaments like Vickers, Krupps and Schneider. A whole series of titles were produced on this theme: *The Merchants of Death*, *The Secret International*, and so on. Details of Sir Basil Zaharoff's murky career were prominent. The argument that the 'Merchants of Death' caused war was a straightforward one: they made their profits from war, and would therefore encourage war by political corruption, planting belligerent stories in the press and so on. As a result of such arguments the League of Nations investigated the traffic in arms, as did the United States Senate, through the Nye Commission. In England a Royal Commission on the Private Manufacture of and Trading in Arms was established in 1935. Interwar peace activists argued that democratic states, linked together through the League of Nations, should control arms production and the arms trade.

Attitudes towards aircraft paralleled these concerns. Before 1914 aircraft were seen by liberals as a technology of communication which would abolish frontiers: free trade would become inevitable, and with it peace. In any case, people who had travelled to foreign lands would not be so inclined to fight their erstwhile hosts. In brief, aircraft realized liberal dreams of internationalism and peace. That aircraft were so widely used in the Great War was seen as a corruption of the aeroplane by war. For example, the London Science Museum's historian of aviation, writing in the late 1930s, while readily acknowledging the impetus given to aviation by the Great War, regretted that it had not developed along 'more proper' or 'normal' lines. He raised the following counterfactual:

> If, prior to 1914, there had been the vision to seek, and the will to secure, international agreement to obviate the use of aircraft for military purposes, the position would have been very different and development in aeronautics would probably have been at a standstill during the succeeding years of war. The ultimate advantages of such an agreement – had it been possible – would have far outweighed the loss of four years of intensive development, and the aeroplane would have emerged free from abnormal influences and could have evolved quietly and efficiently with the sole object of fulfilling its purpose as a great instrument of communication.[4]

He argued that it remained 'to be seen whether in the end the stimulation of the war period would have furthered the utility of flight or, by creating an abnormal background, have hindered its true development'.[5] The faith in technology as essentially civil and liberating remained undaunted, even if faith in humanity proved premature. As is clear from the quotation, the emphasis on aircraft as civil technologies did not prevent liberals from recognizing the use to which aircraft might be put in war. Indeed, aircraft were seen as a particularly powerful weapon, so powerful that, if properly organized by democratic states, aviation could ensure world peace. Thus, liberals were much taken by proposals made in the early 1930s that national air forces should be abolished, and that the League of Nations should have an International Air Police. This force would be made up of fighters, not bombers.[6] Civil aircraft would also need to be policed to ensure that aircraft could not be easily converted into bombers.

The direct impact of such ideas on policy was minimal. There was no nationalization of armaments production, military aviation remained much more important than civil aviation, and no one in government gave serious consideration to the idea of an international air police. But liberal ideas had an impact on public discussion of interwar strategy and subsequent reflections on it. Ironically, the liberal-pacifist view of war and of aircraft may have obscured the actual use of aircraft by the state. The liberal belief that armed services were feudal relics – anti-modern, anti-industrial and anti-technological – implied that they could not develop or properly use modern technology. Arguments about the arms trade obscured the importance of arms purchases by the English state, and the real control the state had over the arms industry. More broadly, the anti-war literature of the 1920s and 1930s may have prevented the emergence of a realistic left-wing analysis of the strategy of the English state.

Aircraft and Liberal Militarism

English strategy was not a reflection of public opinion, or even Parliamentary opinion. It was determined autonomously in the highest levels of the state machine: the Committee of Imperial Defence, the Cabinet and the Treasury. Nevertheless, a liberal conception of war was very important in shaping strategic priorities. But it was liberal without being pacifist or anti-imperialist. It may be called liberal in that it involved thinking about war in economic terms; great importance was also attached to technology, which was thought to be best developed by the private sector. Such a view of war is not militaristic in the classic sense of the term. Thus Alfred Vagts argued that:

> militarism does not exist when armies call for and make efficient, rational, up to date and, to a certain extent, human use of the materials and forces available to them; when they prepare themselves for war decided upon, not by themselves, but by the civilian powers of the state; . . .

> when they get ready for the true future war which is not in the air, but which takes the form of an image deduced from the general economy of contemporary society and from the materials it produces as war materials.[7]

It was in this non-militaristic way that the English state thought of war. That it was non-militaristic in this specific sense did not mean that it did not prepare for war or see the necessity of war in certain circumstances. But since the usual antonym to militarism is pacifism, it is worth describing this approach to warfare as liberal militarism.

Liberal militarism had its roots in English history. We need, however, to explain the persistence of this tradition given that other countries turned to a 'nation in arms' policy. Somewhat paradoxically, it was the deviation from tradition in the First World War which played a major role in sustaining the tradition thereafter. In that war England had put first volunteer mass armies, and then conscript mass armies, into the field. The carnage that resulted, seemingly so useless, horrified not just pacifists but also many strategists. For navalists it confirmed the dangers of a European land commitment; to some military radicals, like Major-General Fuller and Captain Liddell Hart, it showed the need for technology in the form of an expert, mechanized professional army and a strong air force. For the new air force, aircraft provided the answer: for a small investment in strategic bombers one could avoid the need for a large army, and for a large navy.

The influence of the Treasury on defence policy in the interwar years is generally held to have been a malign one.

The Treasury is regarded, rightly, as the most liberal, *laissez-faire*, and powerful of departments. From these undoubted facts several misleading inferences are made. The first is that the Treasury was essentially anti-militaristic, and that it kept defence expenditure comparatively low. As has already been noted, this was not the case. Secondly, it is assumed that the Treasury was concerned only with the *financial* aspects of defence expenditure. However, as George Peden has convincingly shown, in the 1930s the Treasury was deeply concerned with *industrial* aspects too. Indeed, the Treasury limited increases in defence expenditure not for doctrinaire financial reasons (as is usually alleged) but rather because it wanted to ensure that expenditure was in line with what the arms industry could produce. The Treasury wanted to see arms production capacity increased, but recognized very clearly that this would take time.

It is also often assumed that the penny-pinching Treasury retarded the development of military technology. Indeed, practically everything that has been written on the interwar aircraft industry blames its supposedly poor state on Treasury stinginess, and what is seen as the related pacifism of the electorate. The broader picture is radically different. Right through the interwar years both the Cabinet and the Treasury wanted air power and mechanization as a substitute for manpower. In the 1930s they saw a strong Air Force as the cheapest and most effective way of meeting the German challenge, and by 1939 the Air Ministry was the largest spender of the service ministries where it had once been the lowest. The RAF, and aeronautical technology, were thus important beneficiaries of Treasury policy.

We still need to explain why the English state chose the aeroplane as its key strategic technology. Certainly experience in the Middle East suggested that it was a cheap method of warfare. But just as important was a general overestimation of the power of the bomber to bring an industrial nation to its knees. Some of this was due to the propagandistic enthusiasm of the air power advocates, but the effectiveness of their arguments was in part due to the way such feelings resonated with broader currents of opinion in the interwar years. Among these were the fears for the stability of industrial societies and the desire to find new heroes for an unheroic age. The liberal emphasis on cheapness in defence combined in unexpected ways with anti-liberal sentiments. It is to the examination of these sentiments to which we now turn.

Technology and Culture

Before the First World War, the German economic historian Werner Sombart wrote: 'We feel a shudder down our backs as we are watching a flying machine ascend into the air, but never once do we realize that its only purpose for the present is to add an exciting item to a music-hall programme, or, at best, to enrich a few mechanics.'[8] That 'shudder' is still with us; it is a social rather than an aeronautical phenomenon. Before the Great War the public was regaled with stories about a possible invasion by

Germany. The government argued that the Royal Navy would stop any such thing. Then aeroplanes and airships came along, and a long-lasting cliché was coined, perhaps by Lord Northcliffe: 'Britain is no longer an island'. The feeling that this was the case, combined with the fear that a few bombs would be very effective in crippling an industrial nation, was certainly very important in shaping English attitudes to the aeroplane, as has been pointed out by Barry Powers and Uri Bialer. But it is wrong to conclude that the English were afraid of the aeroplane and that they saw it as a hideous foreign invention. Fear of the power of the aeroplane was the product of an English faith in technology. This becomes clear when we consider H. G. Wells. Wells trained as a scientist and from the Edwardian years into the 1940s was the greatest English propagandist for technology. His *The War in the Air*, written in 1908, and *The Shape of Things to Come* of 1933, are best known for their dramatic portrayal of the destructive power of the aeroplane. The film version of the latter, *Things to Come*, released in 1936, is usually seen as a prophetic vision of the horrors of technological war in 1940. *Things to Come* was one of Alexander Korda's most lavish productions of the 1930s: it was directed by William Cameron Menzies, who went on to design *Gone with the Wind.* But the reading of *Things to Come* as a pessimistic film is a very partial one. Wells argued that technical advance made a world state essential, and that it would be brought into being and run by a small coterie of austere technical experts. Wells characterized the chosen experts in a number of revealingly different ways through his career. Before the First World War they were dubbed the 'Samurai' in deference to the modernizing Japanese; in the interwar years they became the 'Airmen'. In *Things to Come* the Airmen use huge bombers to subdue the anti-technological militarists who have taken over England after the destructive war of 1940. They bring the gifts of civilization and peace. Ralph Richardson as the barbarian and Raymond Massey as the leader of the Airmen, played brawn versus brain. The film was a celebration of the 'Brotherhood of Efficiency, the Freemasonry of Science'; the Airman represents 'Wings over the World' an organization which has 'an objection to private aeroplanes' and does not 'approve of independent sovereign states', but believes in 'Law and Sanity', 'Order and Trade' and 'World Communication'. The film was thus a gospel of hope: an aeronautical, internationalist, technocratic nation, a new England, would bring peace to the world. The music was by Sir Arthur Bliss.

Another important theme of *Things to Come* was fear of the mob. The belief that modern societies were kept together by ever weaker social controls was one that Wells shared with many enthusiasts for aviation. The panic caused by small Zeppelin and aircraft raids in the First World War confirmed this view, and suggested that bombing had a very great psychological as well as physical effect. Thus in the 1930s some argued that Germany could withstand air attack better than England because the German population was better controlled. During the Second World War the argument was changed: plucky individualist Britons could take it while regimented Germans would panic once teutonic administration was disrupted. This crass sociology of bombing was not confined to cranks: such questions were discussed at the highest levels.

In opposing the militaristic barbarian to the Airman, Wells was being faithful to the nineteenth-century liberal tradition, which saw technology and war as antithetical to each other. While war might still be necessary, modern war involved the destruction of the old, heroic military ethos. However, while there is certainly much truth in the picture of socially and politically conservative armed forces, technical conservatism must be treated more cautiously. Many military men did not react to new technology in the way the liberal argument suggests. They saw in new technology, above all in aircraft, a possibility of recreating these older, heroic forms of warfare in the modern world. Sometimes the emphasis on heroism combined with a liberal emphasis on economy. Mervyn O'Gorman, of the Royal Aircraft Factory, told the Royal Aeronautical Society before the First World War that:

> It has doubtless occurred to many that, if all the fighting between nations could again be limited by common consent to the use of the short sword of the Romans, 'the weapon of courage', enormous economies could be made, while factors of value to the race, that the strong, the brave, the worthy and the brainy should survive and rule, would still be secured. . . . It would be interesting to speculate as to whether aerial fighting may not in a surprising manner reintroduce a new 'weapon of courage', if not as cheap as the short sword, at any rate far cheaper than the present-day guns and warships.[9]

England's two leading military theorists of the interwar years, Captain Liddell Hart and Major-General Fuller, also looked to the aeroplane, and the tank, as weapons which would lead to short, decisive encounters involving relatively small forces. Aircraft recreated the possibility of warfare between high-status combatants: a 'cavalry of the clouds' – the title of a book published in 1916, like 'knights of the air' much used since – looked after by loyal retainers, cheered on by grateful plebeians. The airman (and the tank commander) would become the new fighting officer-class at the centre of the armed services of the modern age.

It is important to note the aristocratic basis of these ideas: the officer airman was a gambler rather than a prudent investor; he was heroic rather than calculating; a creature of feeling, not a machine. This 'reactionary modernist' feeling was very widespread in the interwar years. It is to be found in the life and work of Colonel T. E. Lawrence, 'Lawrence of Arabia'. In the 1920s he joined the ranks of first the Tank Corps and then the RAF. He saw the future in the machine: the aeroplane, the motor-cycle and the motor-boat. Lawrence did not find significance, according to Christopher Caudwell, 'in the machine as mere machine, but in the machine consciously controlled by man, by whose use he could regain the freedom and equality of primitive relations without losing the rich consciousness of the ages of European Culture'.[10] Heroism and the machine, thought and action, were what Lawrence sought to combine. Caudwell, a young journalist who made his living by writing about aviation in the late 1920s and early 1930s, before becoming a Marxist and dying in the Spanish Civil War, was much more critical of H. G. Wells: he found Wells's 'bourgeois dream-Utopias' stale: they 'revolt our minds', he wrote.[11]

By the late 1930s, however, opponents of fascism began to see a connection between aviation and fascism. After the Sino-Japanese war and the Spanish Civil War, where aircraft bombed essentially defenceless cities, the aeroplane could no longer be associated just with heroism. Bertrand Russell noted in the late 1930s that:

> Government has at all times been greatly affected by military technique. . . . We seem now, through the aeroplane, to be returning to the need for forces composed of comparatively few highly trained men. It is to be expected, therefore, that the form of government, in every country exposed to serious war, will be such as airmen will like, which is not likely to be democracy.[12]

Rex Warner, in his brilliant and insufficiently known 1941 novel, *The Aerodrome*, links aviation, misogyny, modernity and fascism, contrasting this with the life of the village next to the aerodrome. The novel is set in England.

The Right and Aviation

But if elements of the left shared the general enthusiasm for the heroic potential of aircraft, aeroplanes were overwhelmingly associated with the right. This is clear enough when we consider the most active promoters of aviation in interwar England. William Joynson-Hicks, one of the key Parliamentary advocates of air power before and during the Great War was Home Secretary between 1924 and 1929: he was a leading figure in the Prayer Book debates. 'Jix' as he became known, was capable of seeing a Red under every bed, not least during the General Strike of 1926. In that ill-fated action the notorious government newspaper, the *British Gazette*, was distributed by air, as were tear-gas canisters. The *Daily Mail*, too, was distributed by air, from a printing plant in Portsmouth. Aircraft took sides in the class war, as did the still private BBC: aircraft and radio were at the service of the state while the older transport and communications technologies, railways and newspapers, were largely strike-bound.

Jix was not the only right-wing enthusiast for aviation in Parliament during the interwar years, and he was by no means the most right wing. Rear-Admiral Murray Sueter, a leading wartime naval aviator, was elected to Parliament as a candidate of Lord Rothermere's Anti-Waste League and Horatio Bottomley's Independent Parliamentary Group in 1921. He remained in the House as a Conservative until 1945, being knighted in 1934. His name crops up in all the main pro-air and pro-German organizations of the late 1930s. Similarly Colonel the Master of Sempill was a senior member of the Air League, which promoted aviation; the Anglo-German Fellowship, a pro-Nazi association set up in 1935; and the Link, established in 1937, which among other things ran the pro-Nazi *Anglo-German Review*. He entered the House of Lords in the 1930s as Baron Sempill, and in 1939 was one of the hard core of

German enthusiasts who argued publicly for peace with Germany from the Lords. But the most politically important pro-German peer after 1935 was Lord Londonderry, Secretary of State for Air, 1931–5, another member of the Anglo-German Fellowship, though not of the Link.

Lord Rothermere was a particularly enthusiastic promoter of aviation in the interwar years. As has been noted, he had been Britain's first Secretary of State for Air, though he did not stay in the job long. He became a constant and bitter critic of the Air Ministry, especially in the 1930s. He called for an 'Air Dictator' to take control of aircraft production out of the hands of the Air Ministry bureaucrats, and generally went to great lengths to show them up. In 1934 he ordered from Bristol a development of their Type 135 aeroplane, numbered the Type 142. When it was finished, a year later, he presented it to the Air Ministry in a blaze of publicity. In fact, the Air Ministry welcomed the initiative and responded within weeks by ordering 150 Type 142M planes, known as Blenheim bombers. In 1935 Rothermere created a National League of Airmen, which was active in the general election of that year, though it was supposedly non-political. It was headed by Norman Macmillan, Fairey's test pilot, and had among its supporters the Duke of Westminster, Major-General Fuller and Admirals Sir Murray Sueter and Mark Kerr. Rothermere claimed to have spent £50,000 of his own money on his 'air campaign' in the 1930s.[13] Rothermere's air campaign was part of a larger imperialist programme which was deeply hostile to the League of Nations. In the early 1930s he briefly supported Oswald

Mosley and his British Union of Fascists, and his abandoning of Mosley did not make him any less a figure of the far right. It was not just ultra-right politics which they had in common: Mosley had flown for the RFC in the war, and saw in aircraft that combination of modern science and the Faustian, heroic spirit which was so central to his idea of the 'Modern Movement'. Mosley formed Fascist flying clubs in 1934. Several historians have noted that aviators formed a disproportionate element in the membership of the British Union of Fascists.

The connections between fascist politics and aviation in the interwar years may be considered at the level of lesser personalities too. A. V. Roe was a prominent financial and moral supporter of Mosley. Lady Houston, the wealthy widow of a Liverpool ship-owner and Tory MP was very well known as a pro-Italian fascist through her *Saturday Review*. According to her biographer, she had a dog called Benito 'after Benito Mussolini, whom she admired mainly because he had dosed the Italian Socialists and Communists with castor-oil. In one of her letters to the Duce, she invited him to come over here and treat the English Reds and Pinks in the same fashion.'[14] She did not at first like the Nazis, but changed her mind in 1936. On 7 March 1936 the *Saturday Review* carried a picture of Hitler on the cover with the words: 'Heil Hitler! No happier event could happen than a pact between Germany, France, Italy, England and Japan. This would ensure the Peace of the World. (Signed) Lucy Houston.'[15] This was not untypical of the support Houston's paper was to give Hitler until her death in early 1937. The *Saturday Review* was not a minor eccentric publication: it was one of the well-known weeklies of the interwar years. But in the aeronautical literature, and on television films, Lady Houston is still remembered as the generous benefactress of the famous 1931 Schneider Trophy Race. This was not her only benefaction: she offered almost £200,000 to the British Union of Fascists and attempted to give equally large sums to the nation for the air defence of London.

It should not be assumed that being pro-German meant being against rearmament. In most cases the two enthusiasms in fact went together. It is, of course, important to remember that pro-air and anti-German feeling could also go together. Two notable examples were another interwar Air Minister, Winston Churchill, and his friend the aviator Colonel Moore-Brabazon, MP. Nevertheless it is worth stressing that Churchill's position was a lonely one. He opposed not only the appeasers in Government but the active pro-German, pro-aviation right also. Thus, while the leadership of the Army and Home and Empire Defence League (created in 1937 as the Army League) and the long-established Navy League included 'dissident' Conservatives like Churchill in the 1930s, the leadership of the Air League of the British Empire did not.[16]

The politics associated with rearmament were thus much more complex than usually portrayed. Against whom rearmament was directed was not obvious from outside the state machine, where Germany was seen as the key threat. The government was rearming and appeasing Hitler and Mussolini at the same time; it took no great leap of the imagination to see that rearmament might be directed at someone else. The government had after all deliberately refused to aid the Spanish republic against the Spanish right and its German and Italian supporters. Many of the supporters of English rearmament were open sympathisers of Hitler and Mussolini. By contrast, in France the Popular Front government both rearmed and aided, for a while, the Spanish republic. The French right, like the English left, opposed rearmament.

Godlings and Groundlings

What then of the class background and ideology of aeronautical employers, scientists, engineers and pilots? Sir Walter Raleigh's (!) volume of the official history of aviation in the Great War dealt revealingly with the social aspect of aviation. He noted of aviation before the War:

> We were late in the beginning, but once we had begun we were not slow. We were rich in engineering skill and in the material for the struggle. Best of all, we had a body of youth fitted by temperament for the work of the air, and educated, as if by design, to take risk with a light heart – the boys of the Public Schools of England.[17]
>
> An immense service was rendered in those early years by gentlemen adventurers, engineers and pilots, who all for love and nothing for reward, built machines and flew them.[18]

It is clear that Raleigh meant the term 'gentlemen' to cover the engineers and pilots as well as the adventurers. As we shall see, this was a fair summary of the English aeronautical community.

In his discussion of the question of the type of man who should fly for his country, Raleigh noted that in the initial plans for the RFC it was envisaged that only half the pilots would be officers. This was not to be the case because, as Raleigh noted, some had held the 'opinion that not many men of the skilled mechanic class would be ready or willing to risk their lives as pilots'. Raleigh could not openly admit that this was true, disingenuously claiming that it was 'surely rash to lay stress on vague class distinctions'. He claimed that private soldiers had shown that 'they belonged to an Imperial race', and that:

> Courage is found everywhere among English-speaking peoples; the real point to secure is that the pilots of one squadron, or the pilot and observer of one machine, should not only meet on duty, but should live together. That perfect understanding and instant collaboration which spells efficiency in the air is the product of habitual intimacy and easy association during leisure hours.[19]

This was clearly not possible across ranks. The 1916 Bailhache Committee was much more straightforward about the matter. It noted that there was no shortage of candidates for the RFC and that:

> Perhaps the most noteworthy feature of the Royal Flying Corps system is that now every pilot must be an officer. Either he is an officer before he joins, or he is drawn from the class of civilians from which army officers mostly come and becomes an officer on joining. Much importance is attached to this fact by the heads of the Royal Flying Corps, who attribute the skill and initiative largely to it.[20]

It is not just that gentlemen wanted to fly, it was that the authorities wanted the gentlemen to do the flying.

Although the RFC had been formed out of a Royal Engineer unit, it was first commanded by a cavalry officer and attracted many cavalry officers to its ranks. The RFC was never a corps of flying civilian or military engineers: it represented the bringing together of technology with the aristocratic, martial spirit. The association of piloting with horsemanship was an obvious manifestation of this combination. In 1941 the aeronautical journalist Charles Grey, who we shall meet again, started a book on fighter planes as follows:

> An examiner, according to legend, once asked a subaltern in a crack regiment of horse, 'What is the function of cavalry in war?' and the lad answered, 'To give tone to what would otherwise be a mere vulgar brawl.' Alas, the glamour and romance of shock-action cavalry has passed. But its mantle has descended pretty accurately on the fighter squadrons of the Royal Air Force, and in these

days the mechanically-minded youngster, and many an oldster, is as keen on the points and breeding of the high-speed fighting aeroplane of this war as were his grandfather and great-grandfather on those of the horses of our glorious cavalry of the Napoleonic and Crimean and many other wars.

Mind you, I am not exalting the fighters with any idea of decrying the big bombers or the light bombers, or the general reconnaissance machine, or the big flying-boats, or even the quaint craft of the Fleet Air Arm or of Army Co-operation squadrons. . . . But the thoroughbreds of the fighter squadrons, like the finely bred horses of the cavalry, have an attraction for the romantically-minded public which is lacking from the bigger stuff, just as it is lacking from the useful, cross-bred Suffolk Punches of the field-guns, and from the great Shire horses of the siege artillery, magnificent as they were, and are.

The cavalry analogy goes farther than one might think. I asked a pilot of the last war who, in spite of being over forty years of age, and having only one hand and one good eye, habitually performs aerobatics in Hurricanes and Spitfires – of which he has flown as a delivery pilot about 150 different machines – what really is the difference between the two types. 'Well,' he said contemplatively, 'flying a Spitfire is like riding a well-trained race-horse. Flying a Hurricane is like riding a perfect hunter. . . .'

Grey then made his own comparisons: the Gloster Gladiator was a 'thoroughbred polo-pony'; the Boulton Paul

Defiant was like 'the big bony horses of the Lancer regiments'; the Bristol Blenheim ranked with 'the long, rangy (in the horse sense) Walers of the Australian Cavalry in Palestine'.[21]

In the First World War pilots undertook the scouting functions of cavalry, and later the fighting role also. The romantic chivalry of the English public school, and its cricket team, took to the air: it no longer had a place on the ground. Technology made chivalry possible in the air, just as it destroyed it on the ground. Photography also played an important part in sustaining ideas of chivalry. It became the practice on the Western Front, on the death of a particularly heroic opponent, to acknowledge this by returning effects or sending a note to his home airfield, by aeroplane. Sometimes a photograph of a burial with full military honours would be attached. This happened in the case of Baron Manfred von Richtofen, who was killed on 21 April 1918. The photograph was also published in the *Daily Mail*, horrifying some of its readers.[22] It may be surprising that photographic equipment and processing facilities would have been easily at hand, but a substantial proportion of pilots were in fact flying photographers. The millions of photographs they took, with panchromatic plates to penetrate the haze, evoke the scale of destruction on the Western Front much better than land-based photographs.

Technology did not simply give a new lease of life to aristocratic virtues: it also changed them. In the interwar years RAF officers received a broad training over two years. They had to drill, shoot, play team games, and learn mathematics, physics and technical trades ranging from carpentry to sheet-metal work. In the 1920s the first two University air squadrons were established, at Oxford and Cambridge. As Sir Samuel Hoare later said, they 'were to be non-military, they were to be small and exclusive, and they were to be kept in the closest possible touch with the scientific and engineering work of the Universities'.[23] An exclusive Auxiliaries Air force was added. More generally, the RAF was a technical service: in the 1920s it established its own training school for apprentices and a special school for the higher training of engineering officers. A few RAF tradesmen served temporarily as sergeant pilots.

The link between high social status and high technology is clear not only in service aviation, but also in civil aviation. Civil airline pilots were always conscious of their status and were prepared to take strike action to keep it: the very birth of organized civil aviation was marked by such a strike in the new Imperial Airways. In the 1920s and 1930s pilots earned more than most masters of ocean-going ships! When the management of Imperial Airways tried to reduce their status and pay in the 1930s, the pilots responded by forming the British Airline Pilots' Association (BALPA), rejecting the Guild of Airline Pilots and Navigators and its pseudo-medieval trappings. Imperial Airways' management made the mistake of victimizing seven pilots, including the Chairman and Vice-Chairman of BALPA. BALPA had aristocratic patrons, and one of its Vice-Presidents was the Conservative Member of Parliament, W. Robert Perkins (Eton, Trinity College Cambridge, engineer). As a result Perkins led a campaign against Imperial Airways which led to the sacking of the managing director, and less directly to both the resignation of the Air Minister and the nationalization of civil aviation in 1939.

The creation of a mass air force on the eve of the Second World War led to a marked increase in non-commissioned pilots, recruited from outside the service. The wartime RAF consistently refused to make all senior aircrew, or all pilots, officers, despite strong pressure from the Royal Canadian Air Force. The RAF argued that commissions should only be granted to those who showed 'officer-like' qualities; the value of RAF commissions would be depreciated if they were handed out to anyone holding a responsible position aboard an aircraft. It mattered not that aircrew would go to different messes on the ground, or even that the commander of a bomber might retire to the sergeants' mess while his commissioned navigator would enjoy the services of the officers' mess and other officers' privileges like first-class rail travel.[24]

Employers

None of the aeronautical employers came from humble backgrounds: there was no pulling oneself up by one's bootstraps in this industry, at least not in the early days. Of those who set themselves up individually, Frederick Handley Page, Thomas Sopwith, Richard Fairey, the Short brothers, A. V. Roe, Robert Blackburn and Geoffrey de Havilland all came from very solid middle-class backgrounds, from families who could and did support them in their youth. Unfortunately, we do not have a full picture of the tone of the aircraft industry. However, it is clear that Bristol's, run by Sir George White's family, was very superior; de Havilland was a 'true aristocrat'; Sopwith and Fairey both indulged in yachting, and Sopwith was a British contender for the Americas Cup. In the 1930s the Vickers aviation companies were run by Sir Robert MacLean, a university-educated railway engineer. By contrast, the firms run by John Siddeley (created Lord Kenilworth in 1937) – Armstrong-Whitworth, Armstrong Siddeley and Avro – appear to have had the character and ethos of traditional northern engineering firms.

Aristocrats were closely associated with a number of the aircraft firms. Rolls-Royce stands out. Founded by the aviator and racing driver the Hon. C. S. Rolls and the Manchester engineer Henry Royce, it came to be dominated by Lord Herbert Scott. The Scott family, Dukes of Buccleuch, had very extensive industrial and political interests. The Duke of Atholl invested in the Blair Atholl Aeroplane Syndicate, which continued the work begun at Farnborough by Lt. Dunne. We have already noted the work of Lord Sempill as an aeronautical enthusiast and salesman for Blackburn in the 1920s. The 14th Duke of Hamilton and Brandon (1903–73), who as Marquess of Douglas and Clydesdale was MP for East Renfrew between 1930 and 1940, played a part in the creation of Scottish Aviation in Prestwich in the 1930s. He was known as 'the boxing Marquess', was the first man to fly over Everest (1932), and commanded a squadron of the Auxiliary Air Force in the 1930s. It was to his estate that

Rudolf Hess made his famous flight in 1941, hoping that the Duke would act as an intermediary with the English government. Lord Londonderry, member of another immensely wealthy aristocratic family with industrial interests, as well as being Secretary of State for Air in the early 1930s, owned the Percival company, registered at his London residence, 20 Grosvenor Place. Lord Grimethorpe, like Londonderry a coal owner, was the principal financial backer of Nevil Shute Norway's Airspeed in its early years.

At least one ennobled businessman was also involved in aviation. Weetman Pearson, a liberal imperialist MP and later peer, was one of the most important civil engineering contractors of the late Victorian and Edwardian period. We have met him as Lord Cowdray, the Chairman of the Air Board in 1917. After the war he gave the huge sum of nearly £325,000 to establish the Royal Air Force Club in London. Under his son, one of his firms, Whitehall Securities, helped finance many aircraft companies: they bought the small Spartan Aircraft Company, acquired control of Saunders Roe (the company formed in 1928 when A. V. Roe joined forces with Saunders), and invested in Blackburn. They were, however, much more important on the airline side, controlling Highland Airways and Scottish Airways. They later helped start up British Airways, which became the second subsidized airline. An employee of Whitehall Securities, Captain Harold Balfour (ex-RFC and *Daily Mail*), became Under-Secretary of State for Air in 1938, and remained in this capacity through the war.

Scientists and Engineers

The argument that engineers have low status in England has been influential not just among engineers, but more widely. Many of the ills of industry are attributed to this failing. What exactly the argument is, is difficult to pin down, but it can be found in two forms: first that English engineers have lower status than engineers in successful industrial countries, and second that they have experienced a decline in their status since the period when England was a successful industrial country. Unfortunately, this discussion is very imprecise and most of the evidence is anecdotal: we should not take it for granted that English engineers had low status. Certainly aeronautical engineers had high status. They were showered with knighthoods, especially during and after the Second World War. Their professional institution was, and is, unusual in that it started as a Society (in 1866!), like the Geological or Chemical Societies, rather than as an Engineering Institution, like, say, the Institution of Mechanical Engineers. It became the Royal Aeronautical Society in 1918, and remained the only 'Royal' engineering body into the 1990s.

Most of the founders of independent aircraft firms were engineers trained in universities, technical colleges or private engineering schools. C. S. Rolls studied engineering at Cambridge, Robert Blackburn at the University of Leeds, A. V. Roe at King's College, London. Frederick Handley Page and Richard Fairey studied at Finsbury Technical College, Geoffrey de Havilland at the Crystal

Palace School of Engineering. As already noted, many aeronautical engineers who were not employers were university graduates, notably Cambridge graduates. An example of the rarer Oxford engineering graduate is Nevil Shute Norway, who worked on the R101 airship and founded the Airspeed firm in the early 1930s. He later became the famous novelist Nevil Shute.

Before the Second World War having a university education usually meant having money. But it does not follow that non-graduate engineers came from humble backgrounds. Many elite engineers were trained by apprenticeship into the interwar years. An example is Bristol's Roy Fedden who went to Clifton College (a public school) before the Great War. He took a three-year premium apprenticeship with a motor firm, which cost his family £250, and attended evening classes at the Merchant Venturers' Technical College. He quickly became established as a car designer, and during the First World War as an aero-engine designer. In the interwar years he became a very wealthy man – indeed, he may have been Britain's highest paid engineer. He was listened to by the highest in the land, was knighted during the war and became the Special Technical Adviser to the Minister of Aircraft Production. If in the wider world he was a success, within his company his career ended disastrously: he was fired from the Bristol Company in 1942. Fedden saw this as an anti-engineering, class-based attack on him by the White family. Other examples of apprenticeship-trained engineers are Barnes Wallis, R. J. Mitchell and R. E. Bishop, designer of the Mosquito. Nevil Shute Norway of Airspeed, who noted in his autobiography that Rolls-Royce premium apprentices were public-schoolboys, took on apprentices of his own. Thus while many aircraft engineers were 'practical men', we should not infer from this that their social origins lay in the working or lower middle classes.

For those without family financial backing becoming a professional engineer was exceedingly difficult. An example is Frank Whittle. He entered the Air Force as an apprentice, but as an apprentice craftsman, destined for the ranks, repairing and maintaining aircraft. He was one of the very, very few apprentices selected to become an officer cadet, and even then it was a matter of luck. After four years of general duties he went to the Officers' School of Engineering at RAF Henlow. At the age of twenty-seven he was sent to Cambridge University to study engineering, and was allowed to stay on to do research on his jet engine idea. By 1945 he was an Air Commodore, a Knight, and world famous.

The Politics of the Aeronauts

Whittle's class background was reflected in his politics. He was a socialist, like a number of other government-employed aeronautical engineers of the 1930s, including A. A. Griffiths, humbly-born and Liverpool University educated, and R. McKinnon Wood, educated at Cambridge. But amongst aeronautical engineers as a whole this appears to have been unusual: Barnes Wallis and Roy Fedden, whose cases are best documented, were clearly on the right, for example. Other senior men in the industry, were, as one would expect, also right-wing figures and a number, as has been noted, were on the far right. Of course, it is difficult to generalize about the politics of an industry, but the aircraft industry was in one important way exceptional. Its leading trade paper, *The Aeroplane*, which was also read by many enthusiasts, was quite openly pro-Nazi, pro-fascist and anti-Semitic. A typical editorial, that of 1 January 1936, said:

> Thanks largely to the German leader, Adolf Hitler, and to the Italian Dictator, Signor Mussolini, we are now well on the way towards building up an Air Force which in due course will enable us to help them and the United States to meet the real enemies of civilization, the Russians and the Japanese. Perhaps I should say enemies of the White Race, or human sub-species as Prof. Julian Huxley would have us say. [Huxley was a leading progressive scientist]

Support for the dictators, anti-Bolshevism, strong rearmament in the air, and a gross anti-Semitism were the consistent policies of C. G. Grey, editor from 1911. Grey was also editor of the respected annual *Jane's All the World's Aircraft*. He resigned both positions on the outbreak of war, which found him in Italy.

Grey was not an obscure eccentric. To this day he continues to be mentioned in the aeronautical literature as a colourful personality, of strong but unspecified opinions. Astonishingly, in the 1960s British European Airways named one of their aircraft the *Charles Grey.* John Pudney, in his history of BOAC and its forerunners, published in 1959, said of Grey that he was 'irrepressible', had a 'lively mind', and that he was 'at once the most candid and controversial aeronautical journalist of his day', without even hinting at his politics.[25] More remarkable still is the use made of Grey in Harald Penrose's multi-volumed history *British Aviation*, published by HMSO for the Royal Air Force Museum. The third volume, published in 1973, covering the years 1920–29, is dedicated to Grey. In his preface the author notes:

> Because C. G. Grey was the most famous, most pertinacious aeronautical commentator of that time, I have quoted from him more extensively than from others in attempting to portray the atmosphere of those days. Much of C.G.G's perception of the shape of things to come, whether aircraft or international affairs has proved remarkably accurate; but it is the pungency of his comments on the contemporary scene which was, and still is, so enlivening.

In the subsequent two volumes, covering the period to 1939, Grey's presence looms as large as ever in the text. But nowhere in them is there an indication of the true nature of Grey's anticipations of the future or his comments on the contemporary scene.

4. The Many and the Few

Aviation is central to the English image of the Second World War. On Sunday, 3 September 1989, the fiftieth anniversary of the declaration of war against Germany, most television channels had special programmes celebrating the event. Celebrating is the right word since, as Neil Ascherson pointed out in the *Observer* that day: 'What is so remarkable in the British case is how little nostalgia there was, then or later, for the peace which the guns of the *Schleswig Holstein* blew to bits'. Just as remarkable was the way the event was celebrated: TV viewing was dominated by wartime aviation. In the afternoon BBC1 showed *The Dambusters* and most ITV companies showed *The Battle of Britain.* In the evening BBC1 had a play about 'Bomber' Harris, while ITV had a programme on *The Day War Broke Out* which featured a great deal of material on the Blitz of 1940–41. The news on BBC 1 at 10 p.m. openly editorialized on the outbreak of war, and reported a service from Coventry Cathedral, recalling the bombing of that city in 1940 and the bombing of Dresden in 1945. The reporter equated the two bombings without even hinting at the grotesque disparity in casualties: Coventry, 554 killed; Dresden, 25,000 dead and 35,000 missing, on the best estimate.

The popular picture of the air war has been strongly

influenced by wartime aeronautical films, and those of the 1950s and 1960s. All are remarkably similar, even though the wartime films were made for propaganda purposes by a censored film industry. The two most famous wartime aeronautical films were Leslie Howard's *The First of the Few* (1942) and Anthony Asquith's *The Way to the Stars* (1945); both were shown on television in the autumn of 1989. Their tone was quite different from the liberal-technocratic view of the aeronautical engineer and the aviator to be found in *Things to Come.* The wartime and post-war films are about England, rather than about aviation. Aeronautical engineers and pilots are Englishmen; not prophets of a new world.

The First of the Few, which had music by William Walton, was a celebration of R. J. Mitchell, the designer of the Spitfire, who died from cancer in 1937. Leslie Howard produced, directed and starred in the film, portraying Mitchell as a gentle, quiet family man and dreamer, struggling against disease and time; he is contrasted with David Niven's hearty but faithful pilot. The film is a right-wing account of the awakening of England to the need to invest in armaments: it is a vindication of Vickers. It is staggeringly insensitive to the political history of the previous decade. In an important scene we see an illuminated sign strung across the masts of the yacht belonging to the 'painfully patriotic' Lady Houston. The sign says 'England Awake'; the immediate context is the 1929 Schneider Trophy race, but the broader message is clear – she is attacking the Labour government elected that year. Lady Houston's financing of the 1931 race is in the film, but not the fact that she was a prominent sympathizer with Italian fascism, and German fascism too; the opposite is implied. Another example of a film which featured a pre-war fascist sympathizer in a positive way was Powell and Pressburger's *One of Our Aircraft is Missing* (1942). The hero of the film is an aged rear-gunner modelled on Sir Arnold Wilson, MP, who joined the RAF to do penance for his support for Hitler and Mussolini in the 1930s. Wilson was editor of the monthly periodical *The Nineteenth Century and After*, President of the British Science Guild and Chairman of the Parliamentary and Scientific Committee.

Bomber Command was to have another famous film to itself. But *The Way to the Stars* was really about the homely pub at the end of the runway, stuffed with stiff Brits and friendly Yanks: there is hardly a bomber in sight. The film succeeded in creating a poetic rural England within an aerodrome, in contrast to Rex Warner's vision. The poetry itself came from an American aviator, but it is read by an Englishman: the English are too undemonstrative to write such stuff, but good at reading it. The poem, by John Pudney, became as famous as the film:

> Do not despair
> For Johnny-head-in-air;
> He sleeps as sound
> As Johnny underground.
> Fetch out no shroud
> For Johnny-in-the-cloud;
> And keep your tears
> For him in after years.

Better by far
For Johnny-the-bright-star,
To keep your head,
And see his children fed.

Michael Redgrave, one of the stars, felt this poem had a 'strong socialist undercurrent'.[1] The screenplay was by Terence Rattigan, with Noël Coward a key propagator of what might be called the official version of England and the English: middlebrow and middle class. Rattigan went on to write another aeronautical film, *The Sound Barrier* (1952), directed by David Lean (who had co-directed the naval model for *The Way to the Stars*, Noël Coward's *In Which We Serve* (1942). *The Sound Barrier* was a cleverly disguised film about the attempts of the de Havilland company to fly a supersonic plane after the war. The pioneer aviator who owned the firm, played by Ralph Richardson, is a deeply authoritarian character, but the boffin, a minor character, is a kind and gentle man, who wished he 'worked union hours'. The film was made at a time when supersonic booms and jet aeroplanes were national status symbols. But the most famous, indeed classic, boffin film was *The Dambusters* (1955), with a screenplay by R. C. Sherriff. Michael Redgrave portrayed Barnes Wallis as a lonely boffin ahead of his time, parading his gentleness and bumbling Englishness. All our aeronautical engineers are like this, these films say. Anything further removed from Dr Strangelove could hardly be imagined.

The films are elaborations, and very effective ones, of

national stereotypes, which are implicitly, and sometimes explicitly, connected to a broader picture of England: as a nation which is attacked, not a nation which attacks; as a lethargic nation raised to genius by emergency, and saved by heroic, aristocratic pilots and shy boffins. One can sum this up in another way by recalling the conventional chronology of the aeronautical war: evacuation, Battle of Britain, Blitz, and brilliantly clever retaliation. Such imagery hides the vitally important offensive strategy of the English state, one which was at the heart of its strategy in the 1930s: the use of bombers to bring Germany to its knees – as we shall see, English bombing of Germany started before the Battle of Britain. It also hides the huge, impersonal, industrial effort of the air war, both in the RAF and in the industry directed by the Ministry of Aircraft Production (MAP) with which this chapter is largely concerned.

The Delayed Use of Bombers

In the 1930s the effect of bombing was assumed to be terrible and decisive. That is why, as Germany invaded Poland, an enormous planned evacuation of schoolchildren was started. But why did England not unleash its Bomber Command, the centrepiece of the rearmament effort, on to German industry and civilians? The answer is, in part, that England, as well as France, was deterred from doing so because it feared retaliation, even though the *Luftwaffe* was engaged in Poland. On 1 September

1939, President Roosevelt appealed for a ban on unrestricted aerial warfare. The French and English eagerly accepted the next day; the Germans waited until 18 September, but nevertheless bombed Warsaw again within a week. The English and French, who had every justification for starting a bombing campaign, chose not to: a clear decision had been taken by Chamberlain's government, and by the French, not to bomb Germany until Hitler attacked in the West. In a speech at the Free Trade Hall in Manchester on 27 January 1940, the First Lord of the Admiralty, Winston Churchill, told his audience:

> I have no doubt that from time to time you ask yourselves the question, 'Why is it that we have not yet been attacked from the air?' Why is it that those severe ordeals for which we had braced ourselves on the outbreak of war have not been imposed on us during these five months? It is a question I am always turning over in my mind, and, like so many questions in this war, it is difficult to answer. Is it that they are saving up for some orgy of frightfulness which will soon come upon us, or is it because so far they have not dared? Is it because they dread the superior quality of our fighting aircraft? Is it because they have feared the massive counterstroke which they would immediately receive from our powerful bombing force? No one can say for certain. But one thing is sure. It is not from any false sense of delicacy that they have so far refrained from subjecting us to this new and odious form of attack.

> Then the question arises: Ought we to have begun? Ought we, instead of demonstrating the power of our Air Force by dropping leaflets all over Germany, to have dropped bombs? But there I am quite clear that our policy has been right.[2]

From the beginning of the war the government had expressed its horror at the bombing of civilians, calling it terrorism. In a broadcast on 27 April 1940, the Secretary of State for Air, Sir Samuel Hoare, declared: 'We will not bomb open towns. We will not attempt to defeat the Germans by terrorizing their women and children. All that we will leave to the enemy.'[3]

But when Germany did attack in the West, in May 1940, the new Cabinet unleashed an eager Bomber Command on the Ruhr. Bombing of Germany started before the Battle of Britain, let alone the Blitz. In September 1940 Churchill told the Cabinet and the Chiefs of Staff:

> The Navy can lose us the war, but only the Air Force can win it. Therefore our supreme effort must be to gain overwhelming mastery in the air. The Fighters are our salvation, but the Bombers alone provide the means of victory.[4]

In late 1940 and early 1941 Germany and England bombed each other systematically. England was at a geographical disadvantage: its bombers had to fly for much longer distances to reach their targets than the German bombers now based in France, Belgium and Holland. The bombing was intensive all the same. For example, in November and December 1940 Berlin was attacked five times, Hamburg three times, Cologne six times, as well as Düsseldorf, Gelsenkirchen, Duisburg, Essen, Bremen, Magdeburg, Merseburg, and Mannheim. From August 1940 to May 1941 English bombers dropped 20,000 tons of bombs on Germany; Germany replied with 50,000 tons. Another problem was that Bomber Command missed its targets: the disparity in casualties inflicted was huge: 3,000 Germans as against 40,000 British.[5] Bombing did not prove decisive in modern war; for England it proved disastrous. As Patrick Blackett put it in a book published in 1948:

> While the decisive battle was being fought in the air over southern England during the memorable August and September days of 1940, our long-range strategic bombing force was carrying out attacks on Germany, which were as provocative as they were ineffective, and were soon to bring far heavier retaliation – measured in killed or in industrial and civic damage – than that which we were inflicting on Germany.[6]

It is, unfortunately, exceedingly difficult to make a comparison of the *Luftwaffe*'s bomber forces in 1939 and 1940. As was noted in the last chapter, just before the war the numbers of bombers on each side were reckoned about equal by Malcolm Smith. John Terraine gives a figure of 920 bombers in Bomber Command on 31 August 1939; Matthew Cooper gives 1,176 *Luftwaffe* bombers (excluding dive-bombers and ground attack aircraft) for the same day.[7] But while the *Luftwaffe* retained a strength of around 1,000 bombers through 1939 and 1940, Bomber Command saw a very large drop in its bomber force. In September 1939 it could only muster a daily average of 250 aircraft, out of a formal strength of 368 operational aircraft (six squadrons of Blenheims, six of Wellingtons, five of Whitleys, six of Hampdens).[8] The figure appears to increase only slowly through 1940. But one must be careful not to suggest that because these figures were so low no strategic bombing campaign was possible. For the numbers were low precisely because it had been decided *not* to launch a strategic offensive on the outbreak of war. Ten squadrons of Battles were sent to France for army co-operation duties, and thirteen squadrons of Wellingtons, Whitleys, Blenheims, Hampdens and Battles were turned into training units for a later effort.[9] Most of these aircraft were available for the bombing of Germany from English and French bases.

By the end of the war, however, Bomber Command was a mass force capable of inflicting huge damage on Germany. The twin-engined bombers of 1939–41 had been replaced by a much larger force of four-engined craft, each carrying many times more weight of bombs. In a chilling comparison John Terraine has likened Bomber Command to the mass armies of the First World War: England no longer sent its high explosive over trenches in Flanders, instead it was carted on to German civilians hundreds of miles behind the front line. Terraine notes that the RAF lost 55,573 aircrew in the Second

World War, which he says 'has special significance; in the First World War the officer losses of the British Empire included 38,834 killed, and this slaughter of the nation's elite was widely regarded as the most tragic and damaging aspect of that war. . . . by and large RAF aircrew were exactly the same type of men as the officers of 1914–1918'.[10] For the Germans the losses were of a different order: 118,000 were killed in the city of Hamburg alone. The same city lost 40,000 soldiers in the First World War. British civilians killed by bombing numbered some 60,000.

What does the commitment to the bomber tell us about England? It tells us, first, about a considerable capacity for self-delusion, actively encouraged by propaganda. We have come to see English aeronautical history from the misleading perspective of the fighter; the RAF chooses to celebrate Battle of Britain Day but not the continuous bombing operations against Germany later in the war. During the war the public were deliberately misled as to the aims of wartime bombing. The Dresden bombing, at the end of the war, was and is, agonized over as if it were something special, just as Americans agonized over My Lai rather than the routine killing of Vietnamese civilians. 'Bomber' Harris was scapegoated: unlike the other important commanders he was given no peerage, and no campaign medal was struck for Bomber Command. It would be more appropriate to attach the soubriquet 'Bomber' to the whole of the RAF, to Churchill and, indeed, to Chamberlain.

But the most important thing the emphasis on the bomber should tell us about England is not that England is a hypocritical nation, or one subject to very effective propaganda. It is that England was a technological nation. The RAF, centred on Bomber Command, its huge industrial base employing over one and a half million people, and its massive numbers of largely non-combatant personnel, some one million, represented a technological way of warfare. The belief that machines could destroy one's enemy without the sordid necessity of sending troops into trenches represented a belief in the power of machines, and a lack of faith in the martial spirit. Contrary to myth, the average English serviceman had at his disposal a much greater quantity of *matériel* than did his German enemy, or his Soviet ally, though less than his American cousin.

The Home Front

The industrial effort of the war is often subsumed under general treatments of the 'Home Front' or the 'People's War'. In other words, it is placed in the story of the domestic politics of the war: the entry of Labour into a coalition government, the development of what came to be called the welfare state, full employment, the growing importance of trade unions and the politics of the workplace. In nostalgic television programmes the evacuation and the Blitz are seen as critical. It is argued that they brought people together and in particular exposed the middle classes to the realities of the slums, or at least their effect on children. The implication is that the English had been foreign to each other in the interwar years and the English middle class suddenly woke up to its social responsibilities. This led to a wartime consensus to improve the social services and the health of the nation. Of course, the picture ignores the very important economic and political changes the war brought: full employment gave workers and trade unions strength they had not had since the early 1920s. In more radical, and realistic, versions of the Home Front story, these workers joined together in trade unions against the English middle classes and asserted their claims as workers as well as English men and women. In wartime by-elections they voted against the party of the middle class, and in 1945 voted decisively for Labour. Compared with 1935 or 1931, 1945 saw a national split in the electorate on class lines. It was not the middle-class vote that counted for Labour, but a hugely increased working-class vote.[11]

The increasing strength of labour in wartime also had a significant impact at the workplace and on the politics of wartime production. Both official trade union activity and unofficial shop steward action became much more important than in the dark days of the 1920s and 1930s. The aircraft industry had been very weakly unionized until rearmament, but with expansion unionization greatly increased and an effective shop stewards' organization was created. This was dominated by Communist Party members. The German invasion of the Soviet Union in 1941 changed Party attitudes towards the war, and indeed the broader political connotations of the war. In the factories, both the official and unofficial workers' organizations were strongly committed to production and production efficiency. Indeed, many felt they were more committed than certain members of the government and many industrial managements. Before the war such an alignment of opinion would have been, to say the least, rare.

Management in the engineering industry did not necessarily welcome this change of heart by workers. Like the shift in worker opinion, this was also a political question. Management's 'right to manage' without interference from unions and workers was a central concern to engineering employers. The setting of production targets, and the means to achieve these targets, were 'managerial functions', over which the engineering employers had locked out their workers in an important dispute in 1922. Worker complaints about the competence of managers, and worker influence on production matters through joint production committees, were anathema. They were particularly dangerous for management because workers' organizations often had the backing of the state on these questions: to the hard-line employer this raised the spectre not only of workers' control but also of nationalization.

The connections between production and high politics were clear in the aircraft industry. In 1942, doubts about the commitment of the government to the alliance with the Soviet Union were strong, so much so that the Minister of Aircraft Production, the famous aviator Lt. Col. Moore-Brabazon, was sacked for suggesting that it was a good thing that the Nazis and Bolsheviks were destroying each other. His thoughts, expressed at a private meeting, were leaked by an engineering union official. Also in 1942, Sir Stafford Cripps became a potential challenger to Churchill as war leader. Cripps had been thrown out of the Labour Party in 1939 for advocating an opposition pact including the Communist Party. Still outside the Labour Party, he was sent by Churchill as Ambassador to the Soviet Union in 1940: he signed the treaty of alliance in 1941. He returned to Britain and made a number of influential speeches attacking the lethargic conduct of the war, contrasting it sharply with the Soviet effort. Cripps became a member of the War Cabinet in 1942, and later in the year became Minister of Aircraft Production. He remained in this job until 1945, gave open encouragement to Joint Production Committees, took over the management of a number of inefficient firms, and nationalized one of the most famous, Short Brothers. As the firm's historian describes it:

> Stafford Cripps . . . arrived at Rochester on the fatal day at an hour's notice, called an immediate meeting of all personnel and was accompanied onto the platform by the Shop Stewards' Convenors, the management being left standing on the floor; this would hardly have been a tactless oversight on the part of anyone as intelligent as Sir Stafford, and was consequently interpreted as a deliberate snub much resented by the majority of long-service employees, who knew from experience that Oswald Short's rigid discipline and autocratic rule were tempered by his generous humanity.[12]

However, the labour, and Labour, side of wartime production should not be overdone: it was not, as many historians have implied, synonymous with economic planning. The reasons for this equation being made are straightforward and worth considering briefly. Economic planning and state intervention in industry are seen as socialist doctrines, justified in practice by the fact that they were adopted in war. The use of planning by the state is associated with the recruitment of new blood, particularly representatives of labour. Thus wartime planning is summed up as the displacement of the Treasury by Ernest Bevin's Ministry of Labour and National Service; the financial budget is replaced by the 'manpower budget'.

A number of objections may be made to this as a historical account. Firstly, strong powers of control over the economy were acquired by the state in 1939, under the Ministry of Supply Act, before labour in general was in short supply or Labour had joined the government. Secondly, the ideological origins of wartime planning were not exclusively socialist, even in England. Liberal economists recognized that under a war siege economy, one characterized by absolute shortages, the price mechanism could not work. The right saw no objection to the extension of state authority, in total war, to the civil population and industry. Thirdly, the key wartime controls were not those over labour, important as they were. There were controls over other inputs: raw materials, industrial plant and so on, as well as controls over outputs: *what* was produced. The key planning ministries were the Ministry of Supply, concerned with raw materials and army weapons;

the Admiralty, concerned with shipbuilding; and the Ministry of Aircraft Production, concerned with aircraft and electronics. The Ministries of Supply and Aircraft Production, although separate from the service ministries, in fact grew out of them: the Ministry of Supply out of the War Office supply organization, and the Ministry of Aircraft Production out of the Air Ministry. The origins of the key planning ministries are, therefore, to be found in the pre-war armed services, not in pre-war socialist thought. As Joseph Schumpeter put it: 'history sometimes indulges in jokes of questionable taste'.[13]

The Ministry of Aircraft Production

In the 1930s there was strong feeling in certain sectors that the government was not doing enough to prepare industrially for war. Amongst those inclined to such a view there were many, among them Churchill and Moore-Brabazon, who called for the establishment of a civil Ministry of Supply. Lord Rothermere called for an 'Air Dictator'; Roy Fedden for an 'absolute Czar of aircraft production'. But Lord Weir, now Lord Swinton's (Secretary of State for Air, 1935–8) industrial adviser, was in 1935,

> averse to doing anything which would turn industry upside down by creating a war spirit . . . [we] must move to an effective British compromise solution as opposed to merely copying the centralized dictator system.[14]

The Minister for the Co-ordination of Defence, Sir Thomas Inskip, felt in 1937 that central direction was impossible 'having regard to our Parliamentary system. . . . Our system is irksome and to some extent dilatory in its effect, but unfortunately we have to put up with it.'[15] Throughout the rearmament period, until the passing of wartime legislation, there were no new powers to obtain and control supplies: control was exercised through market power and persuasion. The government argued that the establishment of a Ministry for the Co-ordination of Defence met the need for planning and that the established systems of procurement were working well. Then, and since, this response has been seen as a typical example of 1930s complacency. Malcolm Smith has noted that 'the principle of national security was incompatible with the ideological aversion of the time to state intervention: there was not, consequently, the clearly-defined relationship between ministry and industry that was essential for rapid expansion'.[16] In fact, much had already been done within the service ministries to establish significant production branches, and this is now being recognized by historians.

If the creation of the Ministry of Aircraft Production was not particularly significant as an organizational innovation, politically it was exceedingly important. Churchill announced its creation as soon as he became Prime Minister in May 1940. His appointment of his friend Lord Beaverbrook gave the job a very high public profile. Beaverbrook, a campaigning press baron, set to with a vengeance, thinking of himself as a successor to Lloyd

George as Minister of Munitions. As befitted a newspaperman, he put a great deal of emphasis on exhortation: urging aircraft workers to work longer hours (despite the good advice of experts who pointed out that increasing hours of work beyond a certain point actually reduced production, let alone productivity); urging housewives to hand in aluminium saucepans; setting up funds through which workers could 'buy' Spitfires. With respect to the industry, too, exhortation rather than planning was the key to policy. Beaverbrook has had many hagiographers, among them, amazingly, men of the left; they have credited him with miracles of production by disparaging the efforts of the Air Ministry supply organization, and ignoring the confusion he left behind. The subsequent history of MAP, which in some respects represented a return to the pre-Beaverbrook situation, has not had the attention it deserves.

The Air Ministry supply organization was well developed. In 1938 the production and research branches were brought together under Air Marshal Sir Wilfrid Freeman, a very capable officer indeed. Under him was a businessman, Ernest Lemon of the LMS railway, who was given the title of Director General of Production, and to emphasize his seniority, a seat on the Air Council. Under Freeman and Lemon, engineers and management consultants were brought into the Air Ministry to plan aircraft output. In April 1940 Lemon was replaced by Sir Charles Craven of Vickers, who was given the title of Civil Member (i.e. Member of the Air Council) for Development and Production.

A month later Beaverbrook came in, and with him came many new businessmen. Freeman and other senior officials were displaced. Many of the businessmen were associates of one kind or another of 'the Beaver', and went around aircraft factories invoking their master's name. A considerable number appear to have been charlatans who disappeared when Beaverbrook left the Ministry. Not, of course, all: at the top level Beaverbrook operated through Sir Charles Craven and Trevor Westbrook of Vickers, Patrick Hennessy of the Ford Motor company, and Eric Bowater, chairman of Bowater Paper Mills, the largest supplier of newsprint in the world. These men brought a distinctive method to MAP. They believed in the industrialist's way of doing things: they trusted and relied on their own judgement as businessmen, and the judgement of contractors. Medium-term planning, the collection of adequate statistics, and the rational allocation of resources were all neglected – indeed, the statistics branch practically disappeared. Even the longer-term plan for aircraft production of October 1940 was a 'target' or 'carrot' plan, that is one which set its target unrealistically high in order to encourage production. It was only when Beaverbrook was replaced in May 1941 that 'realistic' planning was reintroduced, and systematic thought was given to the co-ordination of production. Only in 1941 were economists and statisticians brought into MAP, largely from the Cabinet Office, to get some order into production programmes. By the time Cripps became Minister, in November 1942, Craven, Westbrook and Hennessy had left the Ministry, but Freeman had returned.

He was given the highly unusual but revealing title of Chief Executive. His Assistant Chief Executive was another senior Air Ministry official who had been displaced by Beaverbrook.

Cripps's appointment was in many ways a remarkable one: he was a member of no political party and his ministerial experience was limited to the lowly post of Solicitor-General in the 1929–31 Labour Government. However, Cripps, unlike Beaverbrook, was admirably suited to be Minister of Aircraft Production, not only politically, as noted above, but by training. He had studied chemistry before the First World War, at University College, London. During the First World War he had been assistant superintendent of Britain's largest explosives factory. After the war he became a very successful barrister, specializing in the highly technical field of patent law. In his mastery of detail he may be compared with another senior wartime minister who had studied chemistry: the right-wing Sir John Anderson. Cripps was a believer in planning who presided over the most complex industrial operation of the war. For Cripps, MAP was not only a vindication of the socialist case, but also an ideal model of a modern, specialized, industrial ministry. It brought together economists, scientists, engineers, civil servants, businessmen and RAF officers – all experts. But, for all the appropriateness of the appointment, it should be remembered that Cripps had God as his 'co-pilot'. And that it was unkindly said of him that one could see the lemonade boiling in his veins. It was such a man who built the aircraft which equipped the mass air force whose primary mission was the obliteration of German cities.

There is another apparent contradiction in MAP which requires comment. MAP had the most complex planning task of all the supply ministries, for aircraft were not straightforward standardized commodities. It was then, and has been since, held up as a model of successful economic planning. But the planners themselves, while recognizing the need for central control of aircraft production in wartime, were not advocates of economic planning as a doctrine. Indeed, the head of planning at MAP between 1941 and 1944, John Jewkes, was to become the leading anti-planning economist of the post-war years, though he chose to attack the more limited planning undertaken by post-war Labour governments rather than MAP. His successor, Ely Devons, was also hostile to planning, and after the war published a detailed study of MAP, graphically illustrating the many real difficulties and absurdities which economic planning involves.

The Growth of the Aircraft Industry

The industry MAP controlled was huge, new and rapidly growing. In the years immediately preceding rearmament the Air Ministry was spending about £6 million per annum on aircraft. In 1935–6 this rose to £9 million, and thereafter to £19 million, £30 million, and £56 million in the last financial year of peace. By any standard these were huge increases. More than fifteen times the number of aircraft were produced in 1940 than in 1935. In terms of weight of aircraft, the expansion factor was thirty times! In 1940 Britain produced some 50 per cent more airframes and engines than did the Germans. Between 1940 and1944 the weight of aircraft produced trebled: in terms of weight, aircraft production in 1944 was one hundred times greater than in 1935. MAP purchases reached nearly £900 million in 1943–4. This scale of aircraft production required the employment of some one and a half million workers. Some 8 per cent of the mobilized or employed population were employed in aircraft production, about one third of the labour force in manufacturing industry.

This is not simply the story of a large industry; it is also about firms which became very large. A little too much emphasis has been placed on the thousands of small contractors who made parts for aircraft during the war. The picture of housewives making sprockets in isolated garages, though too good to miss, can easily give the impression that aircraft plants and firms were small. In fact, many of the pre-war aircraft firms grew at a rate approaching that of the industry as a whole, even though, because of very extensive subcontracting, the average firm expanded much less. The big wartime aircraft firms were huge, and many times larger than the large aircraft firms of the First World War. By 1944 they were employing tens of thousands of workers, which by the standards of 1935 would have put them among the top ten British manufacturing employers: the largest motor-car firms of

1935, Austin Motors and Morris Motors employed 19,000 and 10,200 workers respectively. Avro, just one part of Hawker Siddeley, which itself employed 65,000, had no less than 34,000 workers (44 per cent female) in 1943. It had expanded its workforce from 1,150 in 1934 and 4,000 in 1937. From being in part a builder of other firms' aircraft in the 1930s, Avro became a 'parent' firm: its Lancaster bomber, the most successful heavy bomber of the war, was also built in large numbers by Armstrong-Whitworth, Vickers-Armstrong, Austin and Metropolitan-Vickers.

Another example of massive capacity expansion is the Bristol Aeroplane Company, which in 1938 had three factories at Filton, and a sheet metal works in Bristol. By 1943 the Aircraft Division alone had trebled manufacturing capacity at Filton, managed eight extra manufacturing units employing at least one hundred people, two new assembly plants at airfields in Whitchurch and Banwell, and a shadow factory at Weston-super-Mare. The Engine Division also greatly expanded its capacity at Filton, as well as managing three shadow factories, two near Bristol (including an underground factory at Hawthorn) and one in far-away Accrington. Bristol employed over 36,000 workers on engine production, but its engines were also made on an even larger scale by motor firms in the Midlands: Austin, Daimler, Rover, Rootes and Standard. In 1938 Vickers-Armstrong had two aircraft plants, one near Southampton, making Spitfires, the other at Weybridge, making Wellingtons, In 1940 it took over the Castle Bromwich Spitfire plant from

Nuffield (Morris), a plant which Nuffield had built very slowly and in which it produced aircraft incompetently. Later Vickers-Armstrong operated two more factories, at Chester and Blackpool. By 1944 they had 53,000 workers in aircraft production: Castle Bromwich alone produced nearly 12,000 Spitfires, more than half the total. Spitfires were made in larger numbers than any other aircraft.

Aircraft production expansion was as much about the growth of production of certain types of aircraft as about the increase in size of certain firms. Here there were many surprises. For example, Supermarine, a builder of flying boats, designed the Spitfire, the most successful fighter aircraft of the war, whose basic design was so successful that it could be constantly modified and improved. Another great surprise was the de Havilland Mosquito, an aircraft produced in very large numbers, though de Havilland had made no military aircraft in the 1930s. The growth of Rolls-Royce was associated with one engine, the Merlin. It was built by Rolls- Royce in its original factory in Derby as well as in new factories in Crewe and Glasgow, and by Ford in Manchester. The Ford plant became the largest engine factory in Britain: towards the end of the war it was producing 1,000 engines per month and employed over 17,000 workers.

Failures of particular aircraft also had major effects on firms. Armstrong-Whitworth's Whitley bomber of the 1930s was never very successful, and the firm became largely a subcontractor during the war. Fairey, one of the most successful firms of the early 1930s, produced only small naval types during the war, and a large number of subcontracted types. Shorts produced one of the worst heavy bombers of the war so inefficiently that they were nationalized. On the engine side, Napier, which at its peak employed over 20,000 people, was the biggest failure: their Sabre engine was easily the most expensive and unreliable engine of the war.

The Industry and the State: Conflict and Harmony

The actual expansion of aircraft production has usually been regarded as relatively uncontroversial. Historians have debated the reasons for the state's supposed delays in expanding production but not the relations between the state and the firms. An exception is R. P. Shay, who has examined the means by which the aircraft manufacturers obtained large profits on their contracts. But there were many other questions which divided the state from the aircraft industry, which neither side has wanted to stress. This was certainly the case in the 1930s even though it had been a central principle of policy that rearmament should involve only the least possible interference in the private enterprise prerogatives of the aircraft industry.

One area of concern was the diminishing British share of a rapidly expanding export market for military aircraft. The largest market was the Far East, where China and Japan were at war. However, the European powers, engaged in their own rearmament, largely left this market to the Americans, who in the process became the world's largest exporter of aircraft. Worse still was the fact that in 1938 the Air Ministry itself and the French placed orders for American aircraft. Two hundred military variants of the Lockheed Electra twin-engined airliner were ordered for the RAF, thus establishing Lockheed as a major manufacturer for the first time. English manufacturers were furious.

Needless to say, the most important conflicts were over the Air Ministry's expansion programme. Many of the Air Ministry's key policies met opposition from the firms and their trade association, the Society of British Aircraft Constructors. How capacity was to be increased proved a very controversial issue. Beyond a certain point, firms were reluctant to increase their capacity to provide for short-term production increases. The government embarked on two courses of action which the industry disliked intensely. The first was to place contracts for aircraft outside the 'ring'. On the eve of rearmament there were a number of aircraft firms outside the 'ring', and more would be set up. Some were floated on the stock exchange, among them British Aircraft, General Aircraft, Phillips & Powis, and Parnall Aircraft. General Aircraft was given contracts for seventy-eight Hawker Furys in 1936–7. Phillips & Powis, Airspeed, Folland (formed 1937), Percival and Cunliffe-Owen (formed 1938) were given contracts later, sometimes to make trainers of their own design. Phillips & Powis provide an interesting case. Under their designer F. G. Miles they had produced some very successful racing planes in 1935. They decided to go public, with Rolls-Royce taking a controlling stake. They built trainers of their own design for the Air Ministry, and were admitted to full membership of the SBAC in 1942.

In 1941 Miles bought control of the company and renamed it Miles Aircraft in 1943. It employed over 6,000 people at its wartime peak.

Bringing in new aircraft firms was not, however, the main means of increasing the productive base. In 1936 the Air Ministry chose to pay private firms, mostly motor firms, to build and run 'shadow' factories which would remain state-owned. This half-way house between public and private has remained important to the arms industry to this day. In recent years the practice has been extended to the Royal Dockyards, still run by private firms. In the United States there is a standard term for this: GOCO – Government Owned, Contractor Operated. In Britain the terms 'shadow' and 'agency' factory have been used. The decision to create shadow factories, rather than government factories like the Royal Ordnance Factories, owed something to a misreading of the experience of the First World War. Many 'agency' factories, usually called National Factories, had been built, including three National Aircraft Factories. These National Aircraft Factories produced very few aircraft by the time the war ended, but a misleading official history concluded that their failure was due to the fact they were state-run. They were in fact privately operated! The main reason for choosing 'shadow' operation was a straightforward bias in favour of private enterprise: it was believed that private enterprise could build new factories faster, and that the production experience of private firms should be used. It was also believed that when demand fell it would be easier to close down shadow factories than government factories, and that one could not attract sufficient managers and technicians at civil service rates of pay. Five (Austin, Daimler, Rootes, Rover and Standard) motor-car manufacturers would build and manage new factories for Bristol engines, two more (Austin and Rootes) would do the same for airframes. In 1938 the Air Ministry launched a new shadow scheme bringing in the electrical firms Metropolitan-Vickers and English Electric, as well as the Nuffield Organisation. By late 1938, however, problems arose with the rate of building and manufacture in both shadow and private factories. The Air Ministry considered but rejected the possibility of establishing a government factory. But by 1939 it had decided to finance extensions to established aircraft firms rather than bringing in outside firms to manage aircraft and engine production, with only a few exceptions, like the Ford Merlin plant. By the end of the war the government had spent £225 million on extensions and £146 million on shadow capacity, perhaps £15 billion at today's prices.

The SBAC were hostile to the shadow policy. They felt that it broke promises made in the 1920s to reserve production to the 'ring'. They also argued against it on the grounds that aircraft production was a highly specialized business. According to the SBAC, aircraft production, unlike car production, required flexibility to make modifications rather than standardization: quality and performance were more important than costs of production. But when it came to making modifications and changing types, the firms would prove recalcitrant. They objected to making aircraft designed by other firms, or letting other firms make their aircraft. Fairey did not want to stop Battle production and move to another aircraft; Vickers were very reluctant to let other firms make Wellingtons. Handley Page at first refused to let other firms make his bombers. By the late 1930s the aircraft manufacturers argued for the mass production of established, relatively simple aircraft and for fewer modifications. In the measured prose of the official history of the design and development of aircraft:

> important sections of the industry preferred producing the well established types. It is therefore no wonder that the behaviour of individual firms gave grounds for suspicion that the introduction of new types was delayed in the hope of 'wangling' a continuation order.[17]

Aircraft such as the Fairey Battle, the Armstrong-Whitworth Whitley and the Bristol Blenheim were produced long after they had outlived their usefulness as fighting machines.

The firms and the SBAC wanted a direct role in the determination of aircraft design and production policy. This the Air Ministry and government would not allow, and in December 1937 the government made a dramatic move to neutralize the SBAC. The Prime Minister suggested to the SBAC that they appoint Sir Charles Bruce Gardner as a full-time, paid, 'independent' Chairman to act as the link between themselves and the Air Ministry. The SBAC reluctantly agreed but did not fully understand what they had let themselves in for. They first interpreted 'independent' to mean, as was usual, the financial independence of the Chairman from the industry, but what the government meant was independent of the Council of the SBAC! The SBAC were forced to accept Bruce Gardner as Executive Chairman of the SBAC, to act as the spokesman of the SBAC to government and, remarkably, vice versa.

The SBAC got their own back. In 1938 the Air Minister, Lord Swinton, was forced to resign. Complaints about delays in defence production and about the state of civil aviation took their toll. Swinton's position in the House of Lords was, in any case, unsatisfactory for such an important minister. But SBAC complaints continued. They told the new Advisory Panels of Industrialists (which advised the Air Minister and the Prime Minister on rearmament) that the technical and production branches of the Air Ministry should be downgraded. They called for the minimum of interference by what they called 'departmental technicians', making the extraordinary claim that:

> Technical advances have only been made when the manufacturer and the users of the machines have been able from unofficial discussion to evolve successful private ventures often in the teeth of official opposition of the Technical Departments.[18]

Later they would reject the rationale for the existence of the Ministry of Aircraft Production: they felt that 'the Air

Staff having decided strategical and tactical requirements, Industry should supply the engineering interpretation of these requirements in the form of operational aircraft'.[19] The role of MAP should be limited to co-ordinating and facilitating manufacture. Furthermore they argued that production policy should be decided in consultation with the SBAC. MAP rejected these arguments, and made sure that the SBAC had no authority over the design and production of aircraft. This provides a contrast to much of the rest of war production, where trade associations were granted just such roles, and the strengthening of trade associations was seen as a model for future peacetime industrial policy. Through a neat irony, the government-appointed Chairman of the SBAC, Sir Charles Bruce Gardner, chaired the Federation of British Industries Committee on Industrial Organisation which sat between 1942 and 1945. The Committee argued for a much greater role for trade associations in policy-making, and rejected a role for the state in their affairs!

Another example of friction between MAP and the SBAC concerned a MAP plan to publish an SBAC booklet on the history of the aircraft industry. The project fell through because MAP found the book politically objectionable. The SBAC feared that MAP would bring out its own booklet which would tell the story of wartime aircraft production in a somewhat less pro-industry vein than they would have liked. They were right to worry. When MAP did publish such a booklet in 1947, it was less than fulsome in its praise of the industry:

despite the big increase in their own responsibilities, and in their own real importance in the war effort, a large number of highly individualistic managements were called upon to accept direction and control, in many matters, from a central Ministry. Few people who have not encountered it realize the passionate pride of the keen industrialist in his own organization, and the strength of his belief in its particular way of doing things.[20]

Management and Ownership Changes

In the 1930s, and especially during the war, the government had been forced to intervene in the management of private firms. In some cases this amounted to little more than encouragement of certain takeovers and mergers; in one extreme wartime case, a leading aircraft firm, Short Brothers, was nationalized. Among the smaller firms there were changes in ownership in the late 1930s. With Air Ministry encouragement, Airspeed (1934) Ltd. was taken over by Swan Hunter and Wigham Richardson, and in 1940 by de Havilland. Westland was taken over by John Brown and Associated Electrical Industries. In both these cases new management was brought in. Even the mighty Vickers was forced to change the management of its two aircraft subsidiaries which were run independently by Sir Robert MacLean. MacLean was fired and the two companies were brought into Vickers-Armstrong, the armament and shipbuilding side of Vickers, under Sir Charles Craven. The management of shadow factories also caused concern. The Air Ministry wanted the management of the Speke Shadow Factory taken away from Rootes in 1939, but nothing was done. The incompetence of the Nuffield management at the Castle Bromwich Spitfire plant was such that Vickers-Armstrong took it over in 1940.

But later in the war more radical measures were taken, particularly during the first year of Sir Stafford Cripps' period of office as Minister of Aircraft Production. In many cases persuasion was sufficient, as was shown at the end of 1942 when English Electric, the very successful shadow producer of Handley Page aircraft, took over the aero-engine makers, Napier. Fairey became the first major firm to be taken over under defence regulations: in December 1942 a Controller was appointed to act as managing director and deputy chairman. His presence was resented as he was neither an engineer nor an aviation man. It was in only one case, however, that the senior management proved so recalcitrant that a firm had to be nationalized. This was the case of Short Brothers, which was one of the larger and more famous firms in the aircraft industry. Wartime expansion was beyond the managerial capacity of the firm; the general manager and chief designer, Arthur Gouge, 'being used to shipyard methods, lacked the imagination necessary to embark on really massive production'.[21] During the war the performance of the firm was consistently poor. In 1942 heavy pressure was put on Shorts to discontinue Stirling production and switch to Lancasters, but both Arthur Gouge and Oswald Short, the Chairman, refused. Oswald Short was forced to resign as chairman on 11 January 1943, and a MAP appointee was elected chairman in his place. However, obstruction continued and on 23 March 1943 Cripps nationalized Shorts: Gouge was dismissed and went to work for Saunders Roe.

The nationalization of Shorts provoked strong reaction: as one trade unionist put it in *Picture Post*, 'if a dozen fighter pilots had been courtmartialled for dereliction of duty, the shock to the public mind could hardly have been greater'.[22] In the House of Commons the many hardline defenders of private enterprise were appalled. Cripps was accused of using 'a purely temporary difficulty in production to make a permanent change by the back door'.[23] Churchill was forced to declare that the nationalization of the aircraft industry would require a general election mandate. More than one hundred MPs signed a motion alleging that discrimination against capital was built into the Defence Regulations. Needless to say, the prestige of the aircraft manufacturers had suffered a major blow and by 1944 the SBAC were privately increasingly concerned that the industry as a whole would be vulnerable to nationalization.

The Efficiency of Wartime Aircraft Production

At its peak in the Second World War, the manufacture of aircraft, engines, and all of the components and materials that went towards making them, employed more people than even the coal industry. Much of the aircraft plant, in contrast to the capacity in coal or shipbuilding, was brand-new. Correlli Barnett, one of the few historians to have examined the productivity of the aircraft industry, concluded that although it was at 'the centre of gravity of the entire British war effort', it suffered from the same fundamental defects as the older industrial sectors.[24] He argued that British productivity was lower than American and even than German in terms of weight of aircraft produced per man-day. But Barnett's conclusions, which he admits are based on approximate measures, are open to challenge at many levels. First it is not clear whether the definitions of structure weight and employment are the same across countries. Secondly, Barnett calculates productivity wrongly: his figures for Britain and some of his German figures do not distinguish between efficiency of work and hours of work.[25]

But there are alternative figures. A properly controlled Anglo-American comparison of aircraft industry productivity was made during the war by a senior MAP engineer, Eric Mensforth. He found US production to be 75 per cent more efficient than British, less difference than Barnett finds. But more interestingly, he argued that this difference stemmed from American production runs being longer and factories larger, rather than from differences in production technology or the skill and dedication of management or workers. It is one of the peculiarities of aircraft manufacture that productivity increases rapidly with volume and rate of production, independently of technology used and of the skill of workers and management. This 'learning effect' was first recognized in aircraft production in the 1930s. Mensforth illustrated it by comparing two English factories, identical in equipment and techniques of production and making the same fighter. One produced fifteen fighters per week, the other fifty-five; productivity at the larger factory was twice as great.[26] The productivity price of relatively short production runs was well known, but often had to be paid; production efficiency was not the only criterion in aircraft production. And particularly not production efficiency measured by weight of aircraft. As Ely Devons put it: 'nobody was really interested in the weight of aircraft produced, but in its fighting power'.[27] After the war, it is worth noting, the productivity differential between Britain and the United States widened. Calculations made in the late 1960s showed American productivity to be three times greater than British; controlling for learning effects, it was between 20 per cent and 50 per cent higher.

The second comparison is between the British and German industries. Richard Overy has shown that the German aircraft industry was appallingly inefficient in the first years of the war. He suggests that in 1940 Britain and Germany devoted about the same quantity of resources to aircraft production, while in terms of numbers Britain produced 50 per cent more. Between 1939 and 1941 the Germans doubled the resources they put into aircraft production, planning for an increase in output of between 200 per cent and 400 per cent: they got 30 per cent more. In 1944, after Speer's reorganizations, they produced more than three times the number of aircraft, using virtually the same quantity of resources they used in 1940. So, even if the Germans did produce aircraft more efficiently than Britain at the end of the war, Britain almost certainly produced more aircraft more efficiently for longer.[28] Perhaps this is not surprising. For Goering 'air warfare was a moral rather than a material question';[29] for the English it was very much a material question.

Although there is no failure to explain, it is worth considering Barnett's three-fold explanation of that supposed failure: the small scale of the industry in 1935, the very rapid expansion, and trade unions' restrictive practices. The first explanation has already been dealt with. The second is certainly justified: rapid expansion does bring problems, but interestingly enough Barnett does not note that by 1940 Britain was out-producing Germany by 50 per cent in numbers.[30] Barnett's third factor is the critical one. He gives the strong impression that trade unions in the industry resisted 'dilution' of skilled work: the unions were 'no less obdurate than in shipbuilding'.[31] This is simply not the case. British and American levels of dilution, as measured by the proportion of women workers, were almost the same. It was in fact the German aircraft workers who resisted dilution, until 1944![32] As Richard Overy notes:

> In Germany the aircraft factories were slow to adopt new methods and were permeated by many built-in inefficiencies which it proved hard to overcome. Handwork methods survived through the legacy of the early industry in the 1930s and because of the high degree of skill

> acquired by the individual Meister (the master craftsman) through a long and rigorous apprenticeship. The work-force resisted attempts to undermine the skills or dilute the workforce by using new methods and semi-skilled labour.[33]

Barnett is half aware of this but with remarkable insouciance comments that: 'In Germany the skilled craftsman resisted dilution out of a mistaken belief that it would mar the superb quality of the German engineering product; in Britain they resisted it simply in defence of privilege'![34] This is not an isolated example of sheer prejudice: pretty well all the faults Barnett finds in the British aircraft industry – emphasis on design rather than production, inter-firm rivalry – were probably to be found to a greater degree in the German rather than the British industry.

But the efficiency of British aircraft production, while giving an interesting insight into the comparative efficiency of war production, does not give us a measure of the efficiency of the war effort as a whole. The bulk of the aircraft production effort was devoted to strategic bombers, and these failed to bring about the surrender of Germany. Strategic bombing, while immensely destructive of human life and of buildings, did not destroy civilian morale, or machinery, or sufficient Germans to make a significant difference to war production until the end of the war. Rational, industrial and technological warfare need not work; strategic bombing represented a massive misallocation of resources. This conclusion, backed up by many volumes of evidence, has been ignored too often: we find it difficult to come to terms with the fact that technologies can be both militarily and economically irrational on a gigantic scale. And yet this observation must surely have an important place in the history of technology, and a central place in the history of English technology.

To think of the English state as incapable of planning, of investing in science and technology, or of appreciating scientists and engineers is to misunderstand it and to absolve it from responsibility for its actions. Historians have put governments of the 1930s in the dock. Most have found them guilty of appeasing the Nazis and not doing enough to prepare for war; others have presented evidence in mitigation. However, there is still a general consensus that more could and should have been done to manufacture more aircraft. We might come to a different conclusion: that too many aircraft were made, given the preponderance of bombers, not too few. We might regret, too, that the moralizing opponents of bombers were not stronger. But above all we might regret the irrational faith in one technology which led to massive investments in machines which could not be used for fear of retaliation in 1939, did not work between 1940 and 1942, and often pointlessly destroyed people and buildings thereafter. But in a technological nation like England no one is ever charged with having too much faith in technology.

5. The Sonic Boom of the Scientific Revolution

The term 'welfare state' was first used, in the 1930s, as a pejorative description of the Weimar republic by the German right. During the Second World War it was used by Archbishop Temple as a contrast to the Nazi state. Since then the term has been widely used as a general characterization of the post-war English state. This 'welfare state' guaranteed full employment, redistributed income, provided basic welfare services on the basis of need rather than ability to pay, and extended democratic rights by granting political, social and economic recognition to trade unions. In recent years the right have argued that the supposedly overextended 'welfare state' was the root cause of the post-war 'British disease': under the Thatcher governments there was a deliberate creation of mass unemployment, a redistribution of income (and wealth) to the rich, an erosion of public welfare, and severe restrictions on the freedoms of trade unions. The left never liked the description 'welfare state', since it argued that state welfare was inadequate or was a tool of capital, but it nevertheless identified Keynesianism, public welfare, and state–union relations as the key aspects of the post-war English state.

The idea of the post-war state as a 'welfare state' has had two unfortunate consequences. It has led to the widespread impression that the state was neither a warfare state nor, to use a recent term, a 'developmental state' devoted to industrial modernization. And yet the English state has been the largest warfare state in Western Europe since the war and its devotion to warfare has proved as enduring as its commitment to welfare. But the state has also been committed to scientific, technological and industrial modernization. Much of this effort, as this chapter will show, was devoted to warfare, but it was by no means confined to it. The state supported civil technological development on a scale more lavish than any other European nation: civil aviation provides a good example. Private industry, too, until the late 1960s, spent more of its own money on R & D in both absolute and relative terms, than the industries of any capitalist country other than the United States.

The reason we do not see the post-war state as either a warfare state or a 'developmental state' goes much deeper than an obsession with the idea of the welfare state. As far as the left is concerned, it was only in the 1980s, with the growth of the peace movement and especially after the shock of the Falklands War, that it began to pay attention to the English warfare state. Anthony Barnett, in his brilliant polemic against the Falklands War, coined the term 'Churchillism' to describe the combination of reactionary foreign policy and reform at home that characterized the post-war period.[1] Barnett's target was the Labour Party, and above all its then leader, Michael Foot, the left-patriotic co-author, under the pseudonym 'Cato', of *Guilty Men*, who in 1982 as in 1940 clamoured for war.

Interestingly enough, Michael Foot, who called himself an 'inveterate peacemonger' was, like a number of other left-patriots, a key figure in the late 1950s Campaign for Nuclear Disarmament (CND), itself one of the periodic flowerings of the deeply rooted English peace movement. One might have expected figures like Foot to have analysed the warfare state but they did not. James Hinton, a historian of the English peace movement, has explained why: its ideology, which he was forced to characterize using the seeming oxymorons 'imperialist pacifism' and 'socialist nationalism', emphasized the potential role of the state as peacemaker rather than its actual role as warmaker.[2] After the Second World War, left-patriots cowered before the ghost of Munich and were unable to see that post-war foreign and defence policy was essentially conservative.

But it has to be noted that, like the radicals they criticize, neither Barnett nor Hinton examine the nature of England's military force. One important reason for this failure is that the left tend to study the left and not the right. But another vital factor has been the failure, for ideological reasons, to come to grips with perhaps the key feature of post-war defence strategy: its scientific, technological and industrial character. Scientific ideologues like C. P. Snow, Sir Gavin de Beer and Jacob Bronowski devoted a great deal of effort in the 1950s and early 1960s to demonstrating that science and war were fundamentally antithetical to each other.[3] Even one of the 1950s CND's key books, Robert Jungk's *Brighter Than a Thousand Suns: The Moral and Political History of the Atomic Scientists*, took this thesis for granted: it asked why certain scientists had fallen from grace.[4] But one only had to read successive post-war Defence White Papers, or to consult the R & D statistics, to see that the relations of science and technology to preparation for war were structural and of the highest importance to both defence and the national scientific and technological effort. In the 1950s more than half of total national R & D spending was devoted to defence. This represented some 15 per cent of the defence budget.

Even today the scale of defence R & D in the post-war years is insufficiently recognized; instead post-war science and technology is discussed in terms of two clichés: 'The Two Cultures' (enduring) and 'The White Heat of the Technological Revolution' (failed). But it was above all Snow's 'traditional culture' which supported the rapidly expanding English scientific and technological base. The 'white heat' imagery also misleads. It gives the impression that there was no technological enthusiasm in England or in English politics before Harold Wilson. Indeed the two images, combined as they often are, give the impression that English science and technology were relatively weak, and that the state was not concerned with industrial and economic modernization. In fact, the 'white heat' was a reaction against, to coin a phrase, the sonic boom of the scientific revolution.[5] Wilson contrasted an aristocratic, military and imperial England with a civil, industrial and commonwealth England; less well known is his argument that the first had too much science, the second not enough. Wilson saw clearly what Snow's scientific humanism could not bear to see: the deeply warlike orientation of English science and technology.

Labour and the Aircraft Industry, 1945–51

For most of the post-war years it was Labour which set the tone of domestic politics, if not the dynamics of defence and foreign policy. It might be supposed, however, that the scientific, technological and industrial aspects of defence policy might have been influenced by Labour. In one respect this was the case: Labour kept the Ministries of Supply and Aircraft Production, merging them into one Ministry of Supply in 1946, thus keeping supply matters organizationally separate from the three service ministries and the co-ordinating Ministry of Defence. The inclination of the Conservatives, and the services, had been to return to the pre-war position. However, on the industrial question which most divided the Labour and Conservative parties, nationalization, policy towards the defence industries provides a barely known but very instructive contrast to the usual story. Not only did the Labour government not nationalize the private arms industry, it 'privatized' large numbers of arms plants and stopped a nationalized arms firm from competing with the private sector.

The nationalized arms industry does not figure in general treatments of nationalization or in most studies of Labour's attitude to public ownership. For this reason it is necessary to provide a brief summary. The nationalized

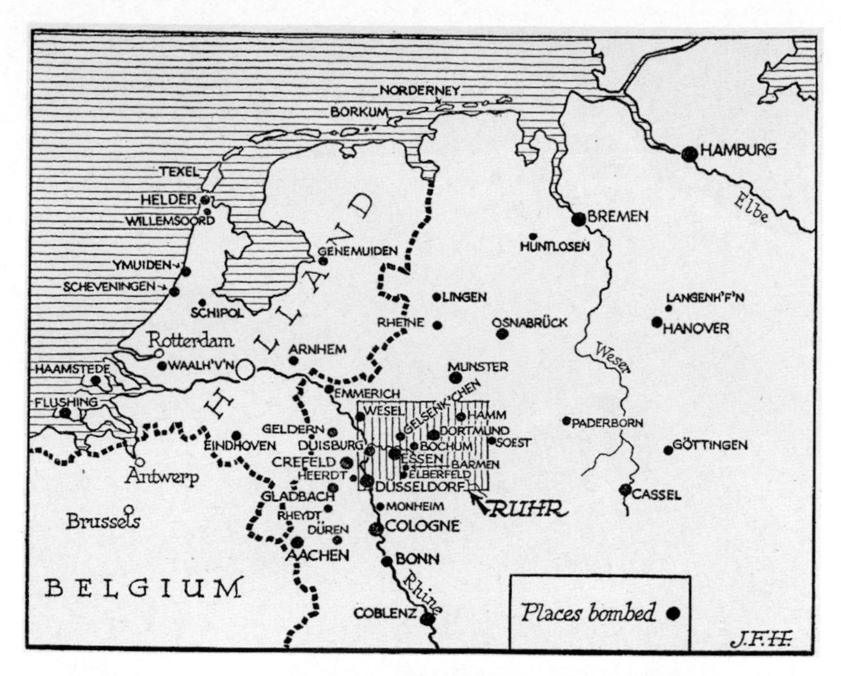

11. (*above*) Holland and Germany showing places bombed June and July 1940, published August 1940 in *Horrabin's Atlas History of the Second Great War.*

12. (*right*) One hour's tonnage of bombs dropped by the RAF on Dortmund 23 May 1943, published 1943 in *Horrabin's Atlas History of the Second Great War.*

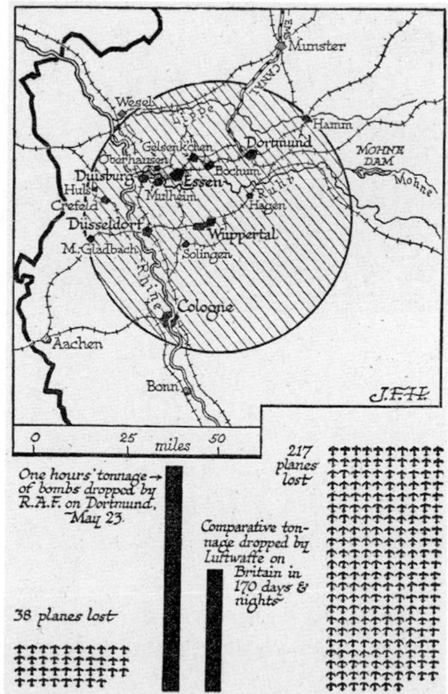

13. Berlin – bombs bursting in the Central Meat Market, taken by 'Willy', September 1941. In 1941 much photographic evidence showed bombs missed their targets.

14. 'Back Them Up', 1942 propaganda poster by Roy Nockolds. Bombers did not fly this low, or strike with such precision.

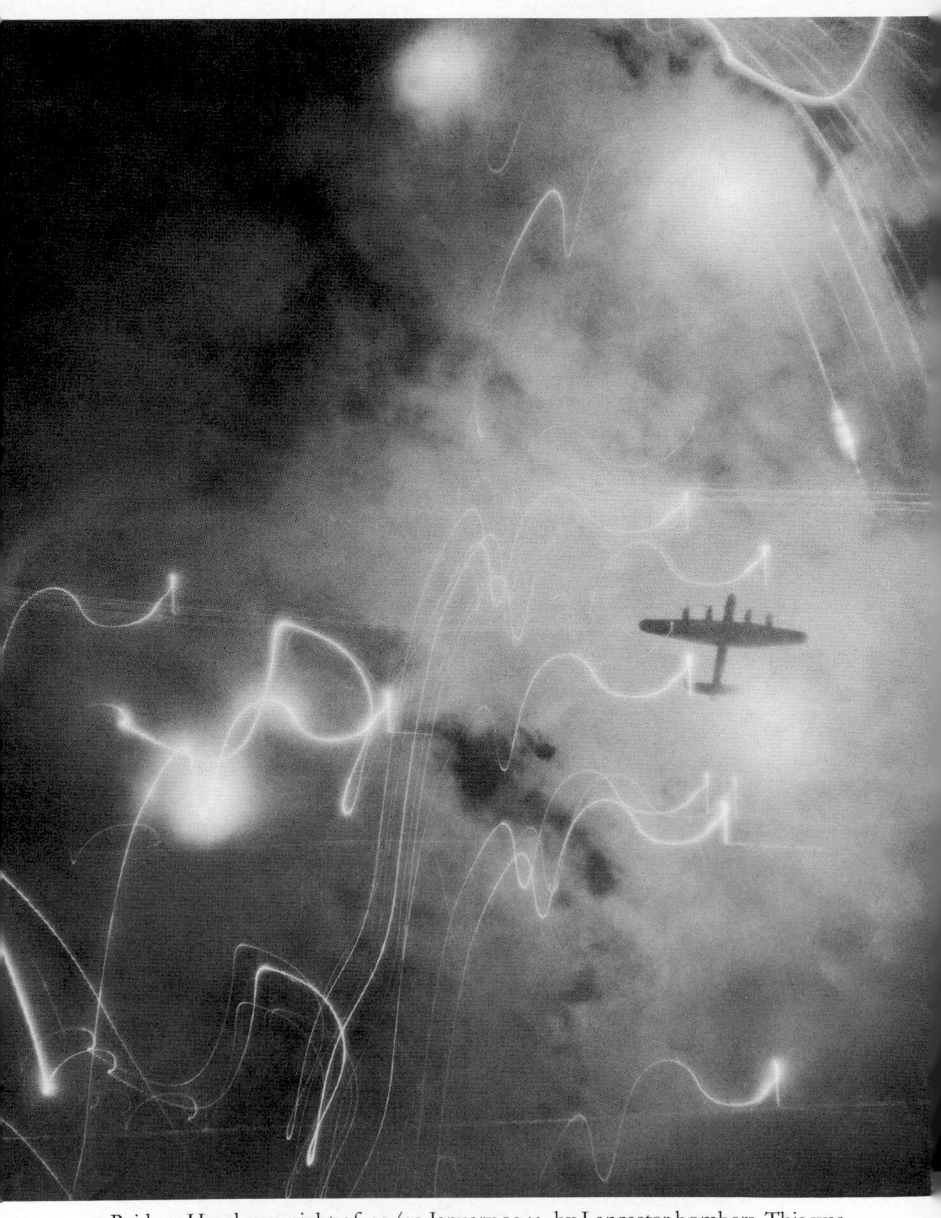

15. Raid on Hamburg, night of 30/31 January 1943, by Lancaster bombers. This was the first time H2S centimetric radar was used. Bomber Command operated by night.

16. *A Debriefing: Member of Bomber Command at Interrogation, 3.20 am*, 1944 drawing by Mervyn Peake. One of a set of drawings commissioned by the War Artists Advisory Committee. Peake trained as an artist, but found fame as the author of Gormenghast and other works.

WHAT IS A LANCASTER ?

Is there anybody here who doesn't know what a Lancaster is?

Maybe you're too busy on one bit of it to stop and consider what the whole affair amounts to.

It's a regiment.
It's an artillery unit, and an A.A. post.
It's a reconnaissance outfit.
It's a transmitting station.
It's a battery of heavy howitzers.
It's the most potent destructor of enemy morale.

ONE LANCASTER IS ALL THESE THINGS.

HOW MUCH COULD SEVEN BRITISH SOLDIERS DO IF THEY LANDED ALONE IN GERMANY ?

WHAT CHANCE WOULD A DETACHMENT OF LIGHT ARTILLERY HAVE AGAINST THE DEFENCES OF A GERMAN CITY ?

HOW MANY AGENTS WOULD WE NEED TO GET FACTS ABOUT A RAID ON GERMANY ?

HOW LONG COULD WE MAINTAIN A TRANSMITTING STATION ON ENEMY TERRITORY ?

HOW LONG WOULD IT TAKE A BATTERY OF THE HEAVIEST ORDNANCE TO REDUCE 300 ACRES OF AN ENEMY TOWN TO PULP ?

SEVEN MEN OVER GERMANY CAN DO MORE THAN A REGIMENT ON IT.

ONE LANCASTER'S GUNS CAN KNOCK DOWN MORE ENEMY AIRCRAFT THAN A SCORE OF A.A. POSTS.

ONE LANCASTER'S OBSERVER CAN REPORT MORE OF A RAID THAN FIFTY SECRET AGENTS.

ONE LANCASTER'S WIRELESS IS A DIRECT PRIORITY LINE TO THE BATTLE FRONT.

ONE LANCASTER CAN DO MORE DAMAGE IN SIXTY SECONDS THAN A BATTERY OF HEAVIES IN MONTHS OF BLOOD AND SWEAT.

ONE LANCASTER OVER FRITZ'S HEAD IS WORTH ALL THE PROPAGANDA IN FIVE CONTINENTS

Seven soldiers wouldn't scare him much. But a handful of British airmen with a nestful of British H.E. bombs can make a million Nazis shake in their ersatz shoes and wish their War was over.

Some day we may send men in thousands with bayonets, guns, cannons, tanks, mortars, shells, scouts, signals, dispatch-riders, transport, stores, kitchens, and hospitals.

That will be to finish the job ; to put the final polish on it for good and all.

But we're on the job now. We want to save time, labour and precious lives.

What's the machine that will do that AS NOTHING ELSE CAN in the whole works—in the whole Universe. Land, Sea and Air, at this present hour?

You've got the answer in your own two hands,—

YOUR LANCASTER

17. Air power theory for workers: a leaflet distributed at Avro works which made Lancasters.

18. Solingen after attack, 14 January 1945. Results of a daylight raid, using blind bombing radar, by 173 Lancasters. Between 1,224 and 1,882 people were killed.

19. (*above*) Krupps works, Essen, a few days after VE Day, 1945. The works of Germany's famous armourer were repeatedly bombed.

20. (*right*) Avro advertisement, late 1940s. Only 15 Athena trainers were built.

industry consisted of plants owned and run by service or supply ministries, known for most of the century as Royal Ordnance Factories and the Royal Dockyards. We have already noted the short-lived Royal Aircraft Factory. The Labour Party never committed itself formally to the nationalization of the private armaments industry but it naturally preferred public to private armament production. When the 1934 party programme, *For Socialism and Peace*, called for the abolition of the private manufacture of armaments, it was more concerned to prohibit private manufacture than to nationalize private firms. In the late 1930s the Labour Party wanted to see public capacity extended. The 1939 party document, *Labour and the Armed Forces*, proposed that:

> The Minister of Supply would be responsible for the existing state armament factories and under a Labour Government he would be under instructions to expand these factories or to set up new factories whenever possible, when an increase in industrial capacity was called for.

The 1945 manifesto contained no reference to the nationalization of the arms industry, even though wartime Labour ministers had argued that a larger part of the arms industry should come under state control.

In the review of policy in 1948, however, the aircraft industry in particular was a candidate for nationalization. Although nationalization was unlikely whatever the arguments in favour might have been, the arguments actually used are interesting. The pro-nationalization argument was that the aircraft industry was an arms industry for which there was a 'moral and political' case for nationalization; furthermore the state was the principal purchaser of aircraft and did a great deal of research; and, bizarrely, that the aircraft firms could not be considered 'capitalist' in that they were guaranteed against loss by the state. Nationalization would allow better planning and co-ordination of resources. The case against was that technical progress required a measure of freedom from control; there was no widespread demand for nationalization from the trade unions; and that the state as monopoly purchaser had all the powers required to control the industry. John Freeman, the Parliamentary Secretary to the Ministry of Supply, argued that in peacetime waste of resources was unavoidable if 'war potential' was to be maintained, but most importantly of all 'any undue centralization on nationalization would undoubtedly impoverish the main tide of technical thought'; he had little doubt that 'the keen and healthy competition which at present exists between design teams is essential to success'. He concluded that: 'There is no reason arising out of the purely physical difficulties of pursuing research and development, and maintaining or expanding productive potential, which requires the Government to take any new powers of control over the industry'. Such difficulties that had arisen in the post-war years were 'either inevitable or arise from a weakness in policy or administration on the part of the government and do not arise from an inherent lack of power'.[6] In other words, the whole issue was regarded as an administrative one in which questions of ownership of property were irrelevant. However, issues of ownership were not irrelevant, as the Labour government's policy of selling off arms plants showed. It 'privatized' large swathes of aircraft production capacity by selling it to general engineering and aircraft firms, though some aircraft plant was in fact kept in state ownership and continued to be operated by the private industry.

But more remarkable still was the destruction of a publicly owned company designing jet engines, Frank Whittle's Power Jets. Power Jets had been formed in 1936, with private funds, and designed England's first jet engines. The production of engines, however, had been turned over to private firms who also started designing engines of their own. Frank Whittle, then a socialist, urged that the whole jet engine industry should be nationalized. In a letter to Cripps in April 1943 he noted that, with the single exception of Power Jets, the firms involved were not 'entitled even from the most capitalistic standpoint to benefit financially other than from the profit allowed on Government contracts'. He concluded that:

> The case for nationalization seems to me to be overwhelmingly strong, so much so that the public would be entitled to raise a vigorous outcry through Parliament if a few private firms were allowed to grasp for the benefit of their shareholders that which should properly be the property of the state.[7]

Cripps, however, nationalized only Whittle's firm, and merged MAP's own gas-turbine research establishment into it. Power Jets became a limited company owned by the state, which Cripps intended should continue to design jet engines and to manufacture them on a small scale. However, the private firms objected strongly and MAP would not authorize Power Jets to design and manufacture new engines.

The election of the Labour government gave hope to Whittle that this decision would be reversed, but in early 1946, the government decided to convert Power Jets into the National Gas Turbine Establishment (NGTE), a civil service organization devoted exclusively to research. As Whittle himself said, it was a 'striking paradox' that a 'Government company was virtually smothered to death while a Labour Government was in office'.[8] Whittle and his team resigned, never to design an aero-engine again. Ironically, the Labour right developed the idea of nationalizing single firms rather than whole industries, as the left urged. Herbert Morrison, who had authorized the creation of the NGTE, announced to the 1949 Party Conference that:

> We introduce a new application of Socialism and Socialist Doctrine. It is called Competitive Public Enterprise. This we should push into new fields and revitalize private enterprise with its own techniques of competition, and, if I may say so, it will not be a bad thing for private enterprise that that should be.[9]

It was not until the 1970s, when the National Enterprise Board was established, that such a policy was in fact put into practice, at the urging of the left in the face of opposition from the right. It was also in the 1970s that the Labour government nationalized the aircraft and shipbuilding industries, creating British Aerospace and British Shipbuilders.

Rearmament

It is sometimes suggested that England's high post-war defence expenditure was a legacy of the Second World War or of empire. It is more accurate to see it as a product of the Cold War. Defence expenditure had fallen rapidly after 1945; by 1948 it stood at a small fraction of its wartime peak, at £1.74 billion at 1970 prices. It was the outbreak of the Korean War, in the summer of 1950, which raised defence expenditure to the levels which characterized the post-war years. Rearmament raised it to £2.77 billion in 1953 and in subsequent years it never fell below £2.33 billion (in 1958), although before 1979 it was never above £2.9 billion (1976).[10] The 1950 Labour government pursued a policy of general rearmament, under both American pressure and a strong feeling, across the political spectrum, that under no circumstances could there be another 'Munich' (an argument repeated, increasingly improbably, over Suez and the Falklands).

Labour's four-year rearmament programme envisaged

a more than doubling of annual defence expenditure by 1953–4. Industrial and technical rearmament was central to the programme: an increase in annual defence production of more than four times was planned. Such an increase was comparable with the actual expansion in defence production in the late 1930s; the difference was that the 1950s expansion started from a much higher base and in a fully employed economy. There were some in the Cabinet, most notably the new Minister of Labour, Aneurin Bevan, who argued that such production increases were neither necessary nor possible. When charges for dentures and spectacles under the National Health Service were introduced in the 1951 budget Bevan resigned, along with the President of the Board of Trade, Harold Wilson, and the Parliamentary Secretary at the Ministry of Supply, John Freeman. All three were ministers intimately concerned with the rearmament programme. These critics were quickly proved right: defence production could not be increased at the planned rate – in each year of the rearmament programme production was less than half that planned. Even so, the 'welfare state' would soon be spending nearly 10 per cent of Gross Domestic Product on defence, having raised it from 6.5 per cent in 1949.

The aircraft industry was a major beneficiary. Not only was its output increased dramatically, so was its share of defence expenditure. In 1948 total defence expenditure was £740 million, and the government spent £96 million in the aircraft industry. In 1954 defence expenditure was £1.5 billion, and £300 million of this was spent in the aircraft industry. Ministry of Supply expenditure on aircraft, engines and spares increased from about £80 million in the late 1940s to £210 million in 1954–5. Research and development expenditure increased from £23 million in 1949 to £60 million in 1954. Employment in the industry as a whole increased from 179,000 in 1950 to 279,000 in 1954, and would stay above this level until 1963. The output of the aircraft industry would stay at high mid-1950s levels till the end of the 1960s. It remained, it needs to be stressed, essentially a defence industry: some three quarters of its output was military even in the mid-1960s.

Aircraft and the New Britain, 1951–64

In the 1950s and early 1960s aircraft were much more than an important element in national and Western defence. They were also a powerful symbol of a new, post-austerity, manufacturing England. During the war, it was felt, English science, technology and industry had been highly innovative. The public and private sectors had collaborated, so had management and unions, and businessmen, scientists and engineers, all for the sake of the nation. Although many felt that during the war England had surrendered its scientific and technological patrimony – penicillin, jet engines, radar, atomic energy – to the American colossus, there remained a strong hope that England could regain its scientific and technological lead. The Americans were felt to be unimaginative and unsubtle; the English had daring and unconventional boffins. This was the scientific and technological equivalent of Harold Macmillan's famous quip that England would play Greece to America's Rome. Today all this looks daft, but in the 1940s and 1950s England was clearly the third, perhaps the second, industrial, technical and scientific power in the world. This was the context of the extraordinary enthusiasm for the Brabazon airliner, the Fairey Delta, and the Concorde, not to mention the AW52 flying wing or the Rolls-Royce 'flying bedstead', a machine for vertical take-off experiments. This enthusiasm for the aeroplane was not, however, simply technological enthusiasm: aeroplanes represented the modern side of the English heritage; England's distinctive contribution to the modern world. Each one carried something of the heroic spirit of the Battle of Britain and the communal endeavour of the Blitz.

It has been said that the aircraft industry was the Conservative Party at work. Certainly, to challenge English aviation was considered deeply unpatriotic. But when the challenge came, in the late 1950s, it was from within the Conservative Party. The cancellation of supersonic fighters and bombers in 1957 meant that in the late 1960s Fighter Command would have no aircraft to defend England and Bomber Command no bombers to carry the English nuclear deterrent. But at least air defence was to be entrusted to English missiles, and the nuclear deterrent would be carried in a partly English Blue Streak rocket. In the early 1960s, however, the Blue Streak was itself cancelled, along with other important missile and aircraft programmes – a national humiliation still remembered today. The disarray was seized on by the Labour opposition who were turning against the extravagant technological projects of the 1950s.

As far as Harold Wilson was concerned, the sonic boom of the scientific revolution was an appalling waste of public money. The 'white heat' was elsewhere, in computers, machine tools, telecommunications and electronics; in technologies which could be applied quickly in industry. Wilson attacked the central pier of technological England.

Many were offended by Labour's brisk cancellations of TSR2, HS681, the RAF P1154 (the naval version was cancelled by the Tories), and by the decision to purchase American alternatives: F111s (later also cancelled), Hercules and Phantoms. The right-wing journalist Chapman Pincher was 'convinced that there is a deeper motive – some festering compost of socialist dogma, pacifism and party revenge which expresses itself in a hatred of the aircraft industry'.[11] Indeed, to this day there is a vast literature which takes these cancellations as indicative of the traditional English lack of commitment to technology and which claims in effect: If only we had continued with the TSR2, especially, we would not be in the mess we are now in. This is itself part of a larger literature which argues that England should have had the Miles supersonic plane in the 1940s, and the Fairey Delta and V 1000 in the 1950s. It is overwhelmingly a Conservative literature, a techno-nationalist plea for technological supremacy still stuck in an Edwardian mind-set. It was against this kind of thinking that Wilson was arguing.

An Industry for Innovation

Ironically enough, the existence of this literature is another example of enthusiasm for technology. The cancellations this same literature complains of were themselves the product of that enthusiasm. They resulted from starting too many projects, from straining the limits of already very generous funding, in the hope that English technological genius would produce aircraft that foreign countries would queue up to buy. Aircraft were at the very heart of the national technological effort of the post-war years. In the mid-1950s government spending on R & D in the aircraft industry was only just under what private and nationalized industries spent on their own R & D. Even in 1959, by which time private R & D spending had increased considerably, the aircraft industry employed 16 per cent of qualified scientists and engineers engaged in research and development in manufacturing industry, and accounted for 11 per cent of all qualified scientists and technologists in manufacturing industry. In absolute terms aircraft R & D was much higher than it had been in the late 1930s, and indeed it probably never fell below Second World War levels. From the early 1950s the absolute level of R & D increased very significantly. Just as important is the fact that the aircraft industry had a very high ratio of R & D to output. In the late 1940s the proportion of government-funded R & D to total output had been about 17 per cent, where it remained at the height of 'Korean war' production. By 1964 it was up to 23 per cent. It was an industry devoted to innovation, if we accept its R & D intensity as a measure of this commitment.

3. Research and Development Spending in the United Kingdom, in £millions

	1950–51	1955–6	1961–2	1964–5
Ministry of Supply R & D*	89	157		
Ministry of Aviation R & D*	-	-	210	252
state-funded R & D in aircraft industry†	30	65	101	110
DSIR R & D*	5	6	15	25
total state-funded R & D*	114	196	289	434
industry-funded R & D‡	24	77	248	328

Sources: *Civil Estimates, Research and Development Table. †Plowden Report, Appendix D, Table I (calendar years). ‡ Cmnd 3007, Summary Table 2, covers R & D funded by 'private industry, public corporations, research associations and other organizations'. The 1950 figure is an underestimate for non-aircraft industrial R & D, in C. F. Carter and B. R. Williams, *Industry and Technical Progress* (London, 1957), p. 44.

Military and Civil Leapfrogging

It is little wonder, then, that so much of the history of the post-war aircraft industry is the history of R & D programmes rather than the history of the production of aircraft. The Brabazon, the Princess, the V1000, the TSR2, the Blue Streak, never went into production. Indeed, much of the history of post-war aviation is the history not even of R & D programmes, but of R & D policy decisions. For example, the wartime Brabazon committee issued specifications for civil aircraft which would come into service in the 1950s. Similarly, post-war defence planners issued specifications in the late 1940s for aircraft the RAF would use in the late 1950s. It is difficult to imagine someone in 1930 issuing specifications for 1940 aircraft and yet ten years became the post-war lead-time for major aircraft. Thus the main combat aircraft of the RAF in 1960, the Hunters, Canberras, Valiants, Victors and Vulcans, were all conceived in the 1940s. The English Electric Canberra was begun in 1944, the SA4 (Short Sperrin) in 1946, and the Vickers Valiant in 1947. In 1949 the SA4 was abandoned, but the Canberra and Valiant went into service in 1951 and 1955. The SA4 and Valiant were 'insurance' bombers, developed in case of failure of the advanced Avro Vulcan and the Handley Page Victor, which were started in 1947.

On the jet fighter side, the Gloster Meteor and de Havilland Vampire, in service from 1944 and 1946, were in production in a number of versions into the 1950s. It was in 1948 that design started on new fighters, the Hawker Hunter swept-wing day fighter and the Gloster Javelin delta-winged two-seat all-weather fighter, and on research aircraft to test swept and delta wings. One of these research aircraft was turned into the disastrous Supermarine Swift. By 1960 only the Hunter was in service in significant numbers; the rest were failures.

As the Valiants, Victors, Vulcans and Hunters were coming off the production lines, the Minister of Defence, Duncan Sandys, decided that in the late 1960s missiles would replace these manned aircraft. The nuclear V-Bomber force would be replaced by Blue Streak missiles housed in underground silos. Air defence would be entrusted to Bloodhound and other missiles. This involved the cancellation of a series of projects already under way: a supersonic bomber and two supersonic fighters. The only new fighter to come into service would be the Lightning, in 1959. Sandys was undertaking a leapfrog, this time into a radically new technology. But the Sandys leapfrog was not confined to missiles; new and very strange aircraft were also ordered. For in the Sandys nuclear scheme of things there was still a role for manned aircraft: the RAF would be a mobile force, largely concerned with tactical warfare, especially in Germany, but also 'East of Suez'. The TSR2 (tactical, strike, reconnaissance) was meant to fit the whole bill. It was to be a multi-role aircraft: a tactical bomber and a reconnaissance aircraft for Germany and a tactical bomber for East of Suez. It had to have a short take-off capacity on rough airfields, supersonic speed, a low-level bombing capacity, a high-altitude reconnaissance capacity, as well as a ferry range of over 3,000 nautical miles to get it to the far end of the Empire. In other words, a single aircraft was to combine a number of quite different roles. The TSR2 was not the only advanced aircraft which would be started in the late 1950s, though it was the RAF favourite. The RAF did not like the vertical take-off Hawker P1127 because its only role was army support and it was subsonic; it did, however, take a liking to a projected supersonic version, the P1154. It loathed the Blackburn Buccaneer because it was naval and was being canvassed as an alternative to the cherished TSR2. Of all these planes it was only the P1127 (which appeared first as the Kestrel and then as the Harrier) and the Buccaneer which went into production in the 1960s. Thus while in 1964 the RAF had V-bombers in Bomber Command, Lightnings in Fighter Command and Hunters and Canberras in Germany, by the early 1970s RAF Strike Command had Canberras, Hunters, Vulcans, Victors, Lightnings, Phantoms (American), Harriers and Buccaneers. Only two, then, were English aircraft designed after the early 1950s.

The story of post-war civil aircraft development was very similar: it was a case of technical leapfrogs into a commercial abyss. Soon after the war, design on a series of new types for the 1950s was under way: the Bristol Brabazon, the Saunders Roe Princess flying boat, the Armstrong-Whitworth Apollo (all cancelled), the de Havilland Comet, the Vickers Viscount, the Airspeed Ambassador, and two small aircraft. In production in the 1940s were many types based on bomber designs: the

Avro York, Lancastrian and Tudor, the Handley Page Halton and Hermes, the Vickers Viking, and the Short Solent flying boats. These were the types that were being used by BOAC and BEA around 1950, along with American Lockheed Constellations, Boeing Stratocruisers and Douglas DC4s. With the failure of the Brabazon and the Princess there were no English replacements for these American transatlantic airliners. By this stage there were three companies designing one: de Havilland (Comet IV), Vickers (designing the V1000 for the RAF) and Bristol (the turboprop Britannia). All three aircraft were due to come into service in the late 1950s. But the Comet and the Britannia were late, delayed by technical problems, and the V1000 was cancelled in 1955, when the RAF decided to buy Britannias. By the time the Britannia and the Comet IV came into service, a superior competitor, the Boeing 707, was available. In 1960 just over half of BOAC's fleet was made up of Britannias and Comet IVs, the rest being American DC7s and 707s.

Interestingly enough, in the early and mid-1950s the government had pulled out of major support for new civil aircraft programmes. It argued that aircraft firms should finance civil development for themselves, and should design aircraft to criteria established by their principal, or at least likely first, customer, the national airlines. It was on this basis that the Trident and the VC10 were designed, the first for BEA, the second for BOAC. The problem was, however, that the requirements of foreign airlines were different. Extraordinarily enough, both the Trident and the VC10 would in fact get government aid from 1960 – aid which only made economic sense if the aircraft had been designed for a wider market. In the event VC10s had to be forced even on to BOAC. By the end of the 1960s BOAC was operating about equal numbers of 707s and VC10s, but by the late 1970s, with the exception of Concorde, the long-range British Airways services operated an all-American fleet. Concorde, begun in the late 1950s, was the last and most expensive attempt to get into the long-range market. In 1959 it was announced that a supersonic transport was a possibility, and the following year a design study contract was given to the British Aircraft Corporation (BAC). In 1962 an Anglo-French Treaty was signed giving the French the leading role in the airframe design and the English the lead in the engines. Concorde came into service in small numbers in the late 1970s, nearly twenty years after work on it started. It has been described as one of the worst investment decisions in the history of mankind.

The Industry

Cancellations, disappointments, failures, should not obscure the fact that the British aircraft industry remained a major employer, and the third largest in the world. In many respects it was an industry which came close to the ideal industry many critics of English industry said, and say, England should have. It was made up of large firms committed to technological change, employed many highly qualified engineers, and had close links with the state. The aircraft industry of the mid-1950s was very different from that of the mid-1930s or even that of the war years. The technical challenges it took on were much greater. Bristol had never built an aircraft anywhere near the size of the eight-engined Brabazon; de Havilland had made only one all-metal aircraft – in the late 1930s. In general, aircraft were larger, faster, and much more expensive to design and build. Subcontracting of major systems became much more important. Electrical and electronic firms, such as AEI, English Electric and Ferranti were major suppliers to the aircraft industry and recipients of government defence R & D contracts for aircraft-related electronics. In the case of the TSR2, for example, the costs of the airframe, engines and equipment were each about equal. Specialist contractors like Dowty, Lucas Aerospace and Smiths Industries also became much more significant than they had been in the 1940s.

Another change from the 1930s was the greater size of the industry and its much higher concentration. In 1935 employment stood at 36,000 whereas in 1955 it was over 250,000. In 1955, even before the rationalizations of 1959–60, the industry was highly concentrated. The top six firms accounted for 80–90 per cent of output. They were Vickers-Armstrong, Hawker Siddeley, Rolls-Royce, Bristol, English Electric and de Havilland. Vickers, Hawker Siddeley, Rolls-Royce and Bristol had been among the top six firms in the 1930s. In one respect, however, the concentration ratio overestimates concentration. Firms tended to have more than one design team. Vickers had separate facilities for fighters and large aircraft; Hawker

Siddeley had four airframe design teams; de Havilland, Bristol and Hawker Siddeley built both airframes and engines. Nevertheless at this level too there had been some rationalization: in the 1940s Blackburn aircraft took over General Aircraft, and Armstrong Siddeley (part of Hawker Siddeley) took over Metropolitan-Vickers' jet engine interests. By the mid-1950s Vickers were out of the fighter market and de Havilland were out of large jet engines. Within Hawker Siddeley, Armstrong-Whitworth and Gloster were much less important than Avro or Hawker.

Even so, by the mid-1950s the government recognized that it was no longer possible to support quite as many design and production teams as had been given work in the previous decade. Many fewer types of aircraft would be ordered, and major contracts from 1957 were awarded only on condition of amalgamation. On the engine side Bristol Siddeley Engines (BSE) was formed to design and build the engines for the TSR2. It would later incorporate the smaller engine interests of Blackburn and de Havilland. BAC was formed out of the airframe and guided weapons plants of Vickers, Bristol, English Electric and Hunting to build the TSR2, Concorde, VC10 and the BAC 1-11. Hawker Siddeley took over de Havilland and Blackburn; the sweetener was launch aid for the Trident. As a result Hawker Siddeley employed 123,000 workers in 1965, making it the second largest manufacturing employer in Britain. BAC employed 42,000 in 1965, but was jointly owned by two very large firms, Vickers and English Electric, and by Bristol Aeroplane which jointly owned BSE.

Rolls-Royce took over BSE in 1966, giving it a total of 88,000 workers.

During the interwar years English aviation and the aircraft industry had been aristocratic and heroic. But during and after the war it became essentially middle-class and dominated by engineers. These changes affected both the RAF and the industry. In the industry, engineers rose through ranks, or were appointed to senior posts from government positions. We may illustrate this by looking at the two key figures in the aircraft industry in the 1960s: Sir Arnold Hall, managing director of Hawker Siddeley 1963–81, and Sir George Edwards, Chairman of BAC 1963–75. Edwards, some seven years older than Hall, started work in the engineering industry in 1928, joining Vickers in 1935. His degree was an external London BSc. Eng. In 1945 he became Chief Designer at Weybridge, and a director of Vickers Ltd in 1955. In that same year Hall joined Hawker Siddeley, having been Director of Farnborough since 1951. He had studied engineering at Cambridge in the 1930s, where he was also a research fellow for two years. He spent the years between 1938 and 1945 at Farnborough and between 1945 and 1951 he was Zaharoff Professor of Aviation at Imperial College.

The firms not only had engineers leading them, higher management was also dominated by them. In 1976, for example, each of BAC's divisional boards had a majority of engineers; 7 out of 12 in Commercial Aircraft; 8 out of 13 in Military Aircraft; 11 out of 17 in Guided Weapons. Most of these men were graduate engineers, the number of which greatly increased in the post-war years. Many were specialist aeronautical engineers. Before the war only Cambridge and Imperial College produced such specialists in any number. After the war many new chairs of aeronautical engineering and specialized departments and groupings were established: at Manchester, Queen's Belfast, Queen Mary College, London, Glasgow, Hull, Bristol and Southampton. Most interesting of all was the establishment in 1946, on the initiative of Roy Fedden and Stafford Cripps, of the Cranfield College of Aeronautics, a specialized postgraduate institution outside the university system. The aeronautical engineers were the elite of the new technical middle-class.

The workforce in the aircraft industry was also highly skilled and considered itself an elite. A very high proportion of the workers were in the managerial, administrative, technical and clerical category (39.5 per cent in 1962, 44.6 per cent in 1970). Workers liked the aircraft industry because of the status it afforded in the community, the high wages that were paid, and the autonomy that the complex production and assembly of aircraft demanded. Furthermore, workers liked the products they made. A contrast with car workers is appropriate: whereas car workers worked on monotonous production lines, turning out ever more units, becoming more and more alienated from the product they were making, aircraft workers were turning out fewer and fewer planes of ever greater technological sophistication. They put something of themselves into each aircraft and felt for it when it first flew. By contrast, car workers were often sickened by the sight of the cars they had made. However, while car

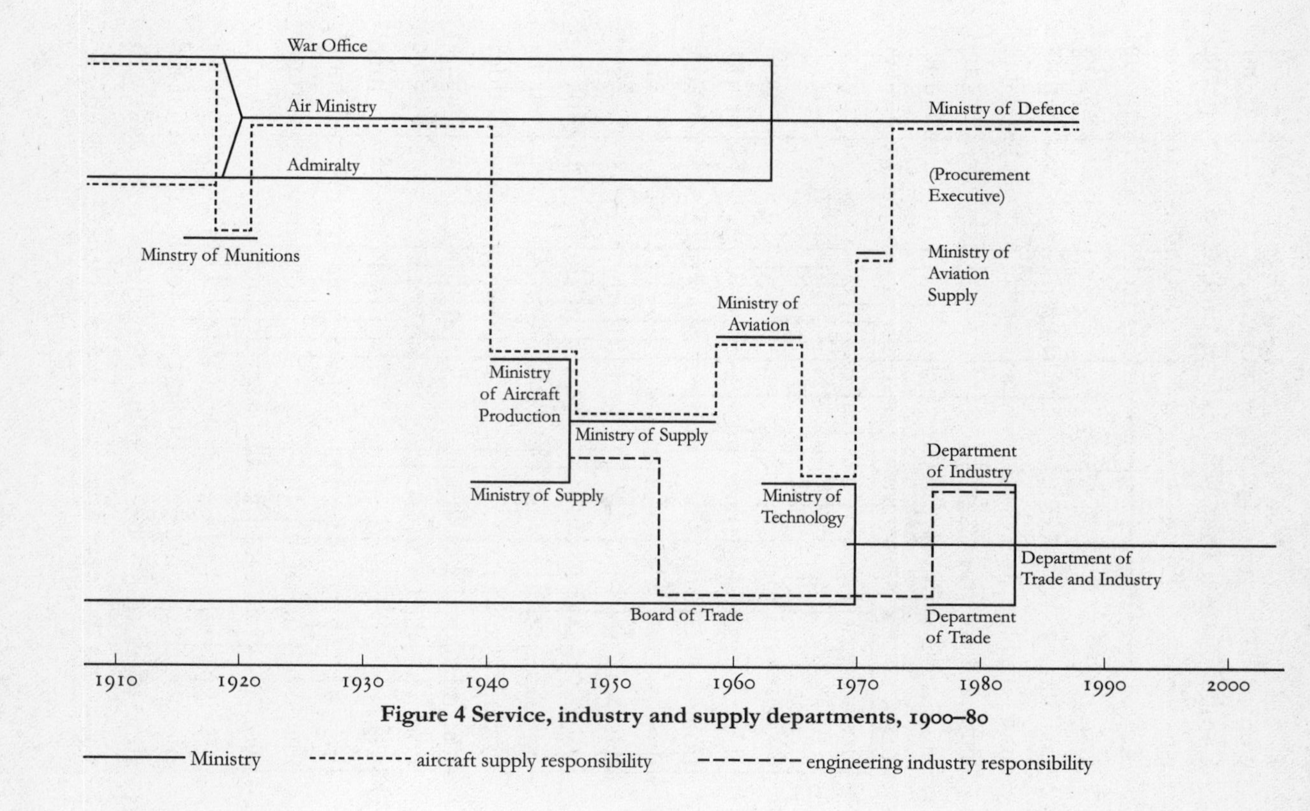

Figure 4 Service, industry and supply departments, 1900–80

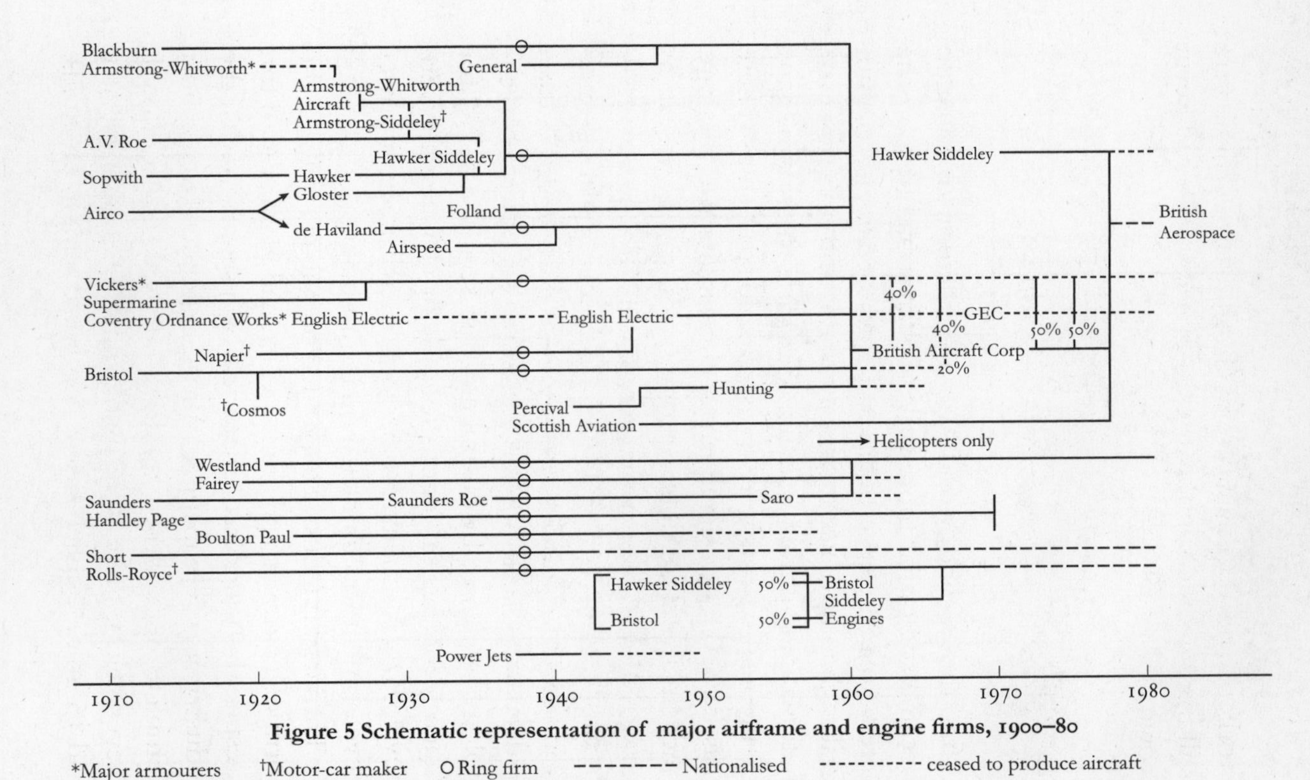

Figure 5 Schematic representation of major airframe and engine firms, 1900–80

*Major armourers †Motor-car maker O Ring firm ------ Nationalised --------- ceased to produce aircraft

NOTE Not all producers are included, especially in the early years workers tended to own cars by the mid-1970s, there were still many workers in the aircraft industry who had never flown at all.[12]

Arguments for Aerospace

After the Second World War the rhetoric of aviation became somewhat more prosaic than it had been in the interwar years. Nevertheless, the idea of aircraft as a liberal technology, as a heroic weapon, and as a hope of national redemption, remained important; though many of these arguments were transferred to spaceships. There was, however, one significant change: military technology, once anathema to liberal progressives, was now seen as economically progressive, because, in the final analysis, it was technology. 'Spin-off' became a ritual incantation, designed to demonstrate that this was the case. Indeed, large-scale publicly funded development of technology, pioneered by the military, was seen as a model for much technological innovation. Major civil aircraft were developed like military types, while civil nuclear power development was modelled on bomb-making.

The aircraft industry depended on public money in the form of contracts and grants which had to be argued for. Despite this there was a rhetoric which suggested that the industry was 'competitive' and independent; its almost complete dependence on the state was played down. Nevertheless, there were many times when the industry had to argue publicly for a continued supply of funds.

The principal arguments for support have the stamp of the English engineers' world view, which may be characterized as nationalistic and technocratic. The nationalistic argument was, basically, that in the modern world it was nations, not firms, which competed with each other. The nation's competitive power was measured by its balance of payments, which was seen as a national profit and loss account. State policy should therefore be directed towards minimizing imports and maximizing exports. Although it was an argument in favour of tariffs and export credits, this general argument was not made: 'protectionism' does not sound good. Instead the aircraft industry presented itself primarily as a national industry and as a particularly valuable contributor to the balance of payments. Aircraft were needed by home defence forces and airlines, and could be supplied by the local aircraft industry, thus saving imports. Secondly, aircraft were highly exportable products, and represented a particularly efficient use of export-oriented labour. Thus in the mid-1960s BAC argued that its exports-per-employee approached £2,000, while the average for manufacturing was £500 per employee. The average for aerospace was, in fact, only £750. These measures, together with value-added and price-per-ton measures, were much used in arguments for government support.

Such measures do not in themselves provide convincing arguments for support since they do not take account of opportunity costs, but such elaborations of the argument were rarely necessary because the nationalistic argument merged with an equally powerful technocratic argument. The basis of this was that certain technical developments were inevitable, and that major economic and social consequences would follow. Aircraft technology clearly came into this category, so not to invest in this new technology, not to take part in the unfolding of its technical logic, was to lose out on modernity. There was another twist to the argument, one which further enhanced its appeal: technology advanced on a number of interrelated fronts, which mutually supported each other. The best way to support this advance was to stimulate technical progress at the most 'advanced' end, namely aircraft. This argument resonated well with the nationalistic argument, for it was assumed that the interrelation of technologies took place at the level of the nation. Thus aircraft were an encapsulation of the technological prowess of a nation and an index of its commitment to modernity. Aircraft became symbols of a nation's manufacturing prestige, the spearhead of its industrial might, a kind of flying advertisement for washing machines and motor-cars. The aeronautical industry was seen as the leading 'sector', itself a military metaphor from the First World War, or the 'leading edge', an aeronautical metaphor, of technological and industrial development.

This kind of argument persisted into the late 1980s. The history of BAC, published in 1981, noted without irony that:

> BAC gained an enormous amount of unique high technology (and prestige) from Concorde, and so did many others of a large network of sub-contract firms all over

> the British Isles. Hugh Conway, then Managing Director of the Rolls-Royce Bristol factory, once replied on TV to the standard complaint that Concorde's money would have better been spent on new schools, hospitals and social services by saying, 'This country has to make and sell things first. It is only when we have sold enough that it can afford hospitals and school milk in the first place.'[13]

Even in 1989, the Deputy Chief Executive of British Aerospace plc, in what he called an 'engineers' analysis' of the problems of 'British industry plc' and 'UK Ltd', noted that:

> It is a truism to say – thanks to the jet airliner and electronics – that the world has shrunk, and with this has disappeared the spare 'headroom' of the 19th Century provided by unexplored or subjugated territories. To help clear the mind I find it a useful working hypothesis to assume that in the second half of the 20th Century the pressures of rivalry between vigorous nations are translated into vigorous economic aggression, with the military spearhead of 50 years ago replaced by the competitive cutting edge of high-technology, excellent quality and high differentiation in the market, supported by continual improvement in productivity and reduction in manufacturing costs.[14]

It is ironic that British Aerospace, and the electronics industry, was and remains highly dependent on military sales, both at home and abroad.

The English State, Technology and Industry

One of the favourite arguments made by English engineers about the English state is that, being dominated by Oxbridge arts graduates and a mean Treasury, it has been incapable of understanding, much less supporting, technology and industry. This view is not confined to engineers: the political scientist Andrew Gamble has argued that

> National political economy has always been relatively weak in Britain – there has never, for example, been a permanent government department to speak for and represent the interests of the national economy and national industry. Mosley's remodelled executive was rejected, Labour's Ministry of Economic Affairs (1947) and the Department of Economic Affairs (1964) did not survive.[15]

Gamble is echoing the standard view to be found in most analyses of government–industry relations and the 'British decline'. And yet, as we have seen, the state did support the aircraft industry and technology to an extraordinary extent. This support was given by departments of state deeply committed to national industries and technologies.

These departments are, unfortunately, barely known to students of the history of scientific, technological, industrial or economic policy. It has been noted that the key wartime industry ministries were the Ministry of Aircraft Production and the Ministry of Supply and that in 1946 they were merged into what was still called the Ministry of Supply. In 1959 its Army supply functions were transferred to the War Office and it was renamed the Ministry of Aviation. This huge Ministry was merged into the Ministry of Technology (Mintech) in 1967, re-emerged briefly as the Ministry of Aviation Supply, and found its final resting place as part of the Ministry of Defence. With the very interesting exceptions of the Ministry of Supply between 1945 and 1954 and the Ministry of Technology, these departments were overwhelmingly concerned with supply to the armed services. Until the absorption of supply functions into the Ministry of Defence it was argued that separate supply ministries were required because of the complexity and importance of the scientific, technological and industrial aspects of defence. Defence supply involved, in practice or potentially, a substantial proportion of the nation's scientific, technological and industrial capacity. Take the Ministry of Aviation in the early 1960s. It was a vast organization, responsible for aeronautical and electronic R & D, procurement of aircraft and much electronics for the armed services, civil airports and air traffic control. As well as financing R & D in industry, it had seven major research and development establishments of its own: the Royal Aircraft Establishment, the National Gas Turbine Establishment, the Aeroplane and Armament Experimental Establishment, the Royal Radar Establishment, the Explosives Research and Development Establishment, the Rocket

Propulsion Establishment, and the Signals Research and Development Establishment. Its total R & D spending in 1961–2 was almost the same as that of private and nationalized industry.

It is little wonder that those who wanted a national technological-industrial strategy should look to the supply departments both for expertise and for a model. For example, during the war Cripps argued not only for the continued existence of supply ministries, but for these becoming the main agents of industrial modernization and employment creation. The Ministry of Supply between 1945 and 1954 was indeed in many ways *the* ministry for science, technology and heavy industry. However, it progressively lost civil functions so that by the late 1950s it was concerned almost exclusively with supply. Even so it still attracted attention as the basis of an alternative industry ministry. Aubrey Jones, the Conservative Minister of Supply between 1957 and 1959, suggested his ministry be converted into a Ministry of Technology

> to facilitate the transfer of knowledge from the military to the civil field; and to utilize the expertise developed in the placing of military research and development contracts to put it also at the disposal of civil industry.[16]

Such a policy was opposed by service departments, and other ministers, and Jones resigned in 1959. The Ministry of Aviation was formed and it was this which Harold Wilson intended to convert into an industry ministry. First, however, Wilson established a small Ministry of

Technology responsible for atomic energy, the National Research and Development Corporation (which Wilson had created in 1948), and the industrial sections of the former Department of Scientific and Industrial Research; in addition it was given a sponsorship role for so-called 'bridgehead industries': machine tools, computers, electronics and telecommunications. It was not until 1967 that the Ministry of Technology and the much larger Ministry of Aviation were merged. Into this already huge ministry he added many of the Board of Trade's functions, the Ministry of Fuel and Power and the Industrial Reorganisation Corporation. This new superministry, unfortunately still called the Ministry of Technology, was remarkable because of its size and range of responsibilities, from practically all civil industrial policy to the bulk of defence R & D and procurement.

The reasons why 'Mintech' (the Russian abbreviation is significant even though the model was MacNamara's Pentagon) has been misunderstood are not hard to find. Its very name has misled and it has tended to be seen as the organizational embodiment of the supposedly insincere rhetoric of the 'white heat'. But, as we have seen, there was much more to Wilson's rhetoric than he is given credit for. Wilson had been very well aware, since the 1940s, of the importance of the supply ministries to technology and industry and their distinctive policies. He had argued in 1950 for Labour to pursue a general industrial policy based on the practices of the supply departments rather than those of the Board of Trade, which he came to despise. Of course, Wilson was later to be very critical of the policies of the Ministry of Aviation, but he recognized its interventionist expertise and its control of the commanding heights of English technology. By bringing Aviation and Mintech together he aimed to bring Aviation under control and to transfer expertise and resources from defence to civil R & D. There was in fact a significant reduction in defence R & D under the Labour government, but by the end of the 1960s, coinciding with the decision to pull out from East of Suez, it was decided that defence R & D should increase.

Mintech did not survive the election of the Conservative government in 1970. The remnants of the Board of Trade were merged by Edward Heath into the civil side of Mintech to form a Department of Trade and Industry, while the defence side made its way into the newly formed Procurement Executive of the Ministry of Defence. The cobbler was told to stick to his gold-plated last.

Many have argued, like Harold Wilson, that the orientation of English science and technology towards defence, and towards long-range 'prestige' civil projects was *the* problem of post-war English science, technology and industry. That case is a very strong one, but it should be carefully made. It should not be confused with the argument that the English elite were anti-scientific and anti-industrial, since it was the English elite which wanted its armed services to be armed with modern technology. Neither should the idea that civil technologies were developed for purely 'prestige' reasons be taken too seriously: civil aircraft, and nuclear power, were developed because it was genuinely believed that these would be the technologies of the future, and that England would benefit economically from being strong in them. We should not forget, either, that many English scientists and engineers wanted, and still want, to work on aircraft and nuclear power. But above all we should remember that in the 1960s a very serious attempt was made to redirect state support for R & D away from the defence sector to the civil sector, and away from long-range to short-term projects. This was not idle rhetoric: a major reorganization of the machinery of government for industrial policy and defence procurement was undertaken. This gave England an Industry Ministry of much greater scope than any other in the capitalist world; Japan's much-vaunted MITI was a minnow by comparison.

6. Conclusion

Progress stalks with warhead and prosthesis,
stopwatch in hand, and glory in its heart.

Karl Kraus[1]

In telling the story of England and the Aeroplane it has been necessary to point out many gaps between rhetoric and reality. What then has been the rhetoric of aviation since? In 1988 BBC Television broadcast a major twelve-part history of aviation. It was appropriately called *Reaching for the Skies* and was narrated by Sir Anthony Quayle, also known for his broadcasts for the Conservative Party. It consisted of little more than a series of now leaden banalities about 'the quest for speed' and 'hero pilots'. For the series, aircraft were civil, liberating, heroic, individual – the physical expression of a desire to make real 'the dream of flight' or as Ronald Reagan put it, quoting a Second World War aviator, 'to touch the face of God'. Neither television nor aircraft can be blamed for inducing this blacking out of critical faculties. That *Reaching for the Skies* was nostalgic and confused tells us of a much broader failure to come to grips with technology.

The owl of Minerva may only fly at dusk, but cynics and paranoiacs get to work a little faster. In 1944 George

Orwell was struck, after reading 'a batch of rather shallowly optimistic "progressive" books', by the

> automatic way in which people go on repeating certain phrases which were fashionable before 1914. Two great favourites are the 'abolition of distance' and the 'disappearance of frontiers'. I do not know how often I have met with statements that 'the aeroplane and the radio have abolished distance' and 'all parts of the world are now interdependent'. Actually the effect of modern inventions has been to increase nationalism, to make travel enormously more difficult, to cut down the means of communication between one country and another.[2]

For Orwell it was 'only since the aeroplane became a serious weapon that frontiers have become definitely impassable'.[3] That Orwell should have seen through the Newspeak of technological progressivism comes as no surprise, but it is worth noting how rare this is. England does not have a tradition of serious analysis or critique of technology, unlike Germany, and to a lesser extent France and the United States. It is significant that it was a technically trained American, Thomas Pynchon, who wrote the most compelling novel on England, Germany and technology in the Second World War. For Pynchon the almost unfathomable gap between rhetoric and reality was central: the Rocket's 'symmetries, its latencies, the *cuteness* of it enchanted and seduced us while the real Text persisted, somewhere else, in its darkness, our darkness.'[4] What postwar English novels, excepting perhaps *Nineteen Eighty Four* and J. G. Ballard's *Empire of the Sun*, say anything about this very real darkness?

The hidden English text is an industrial, technological and political story radically different from the usual one. As this essay has shown, England was a technological and militant nation. That story is hidden not just by the cuteness of the English aeroplane but by a deeply ingrained national myth about the niceness and decency of England, a myth which, ironically, was fostered by George Orwell. That mythical picture of England was the result of wartime films, broadcasts and books but is still with us today. This is also the picture of England which many critics accept: they, too, have fallen for the story. C. P. Snow's attacks on the 'traditional culture', Martin Wiener's contempt for the anti-industrial spirit, Correlli Barnett's charge against the anti-militarist and anti-technocratic wimps are all tilts at propaganda images.

But the problems with these, and other, technocratic critiques of England run far deeper than this. First, these writings systematically deny the existence of any technocratic tradition in England: only the anti-technocratic stand exists. Second, they see the battle as one between a northern provincial, scientific, industrial and modernizing middle-class, and a southern metropolitan, literary and nostalgic aristocracy. Unassuming, moral scientists from the north had the future in their bones; southern literary types were immoral nostalgics. The battle was lost, the argument goes: science never penetrated English culture; science, industry and state have not been linked in England as in Other Countries.

These stories are left-overs from the nineteenth century, and not surprisingly, are incapable of helping us come to grips with the twentieth century when English science, technology and industry were inextricably linked to metropolitan power. Part of the story of twentieth-century English science, technology and industry must be the way English technocrats played out their fantasies: the dream of cheap technological war that would bring everlasting peace; the dream that English brain power would triumph where brawn could not. What technocrats cannot do is come to terms with the failure of many of these programmes: that is why they so systematically ignore or misrepresent them. For it is not necessarily the case that technological and industrial warfare is dramatically superior to less equipment-intensive alternatives, as we have seen. Neither is it the case that investments in R & D need lead to economic success.

This is not to say that science and technology are not important in warfare or in economic growth. They are: that we know. But we do not know how important they are, or how their importance has changed over time, and much more besides. But it is because of the importance of science and technology in English warfare, and in English economic life, in the twentieth century, not because of its supposed unimportance, that we need to study the history of twentieth-century English science and technology. To do so at all adequately we need to be rid of the myths that swamp discussion.

Further Reading

This bibliography is intended both to indicate some of the sources used and to suggest further reading on topics related to the themes of this book. For simplicity, books and articles are cited more than once if appropriate. Place of publication is London unless otherwise indicated.

England, Decline, Technology

A. J. P. Taylor, *English History 1914–1945* (Oxford, 1965) is especially interesting because the author, who was involved in the CND, was very critical of strategic bombing but, while making much of its historical roots, he leaves out the story of Bomber Command between 1939 and 1942. Taylor went on to write a biography of his friend, *Beaverbrook* (1972). A very different picture of England and Englishness may be found in Anthony Barnett, *Iron Britannia* (1982) and Tom Nairn, *The Enchanted Glass: Britain and its Monarchy* (1988). Raphael Samuel (ed.), *Patriotism: The Making and Unmaking of British National Identity*, 3 vols (1989), is another example of socialist concern with what it is to be English, but it concentrates on the left, not the right.

The declinist literature is vast but Martin Wiener, *English Culture and the Decline of the Industrial Spirit 1850–1980* (Cambridge, 1981) and Correlli Barnett, *The Audit of War: The Illusion and Reality of Britain as a Great Nation* (1986) are particularly influential works. Barnett's book stands out as an example of declinism and inverted

Whiggism; see my 'The Prophet Militant and Industrial: The Pecularities of Correlli Barnett' in *Twentieth Century British History*, 2 (1991), pp. 360–79. Andrew Gamble, *Britain in Decline*, 3rd edn (1990), S. Newton and D. Porter, *Modernisation Frustrated: The Politics of Industrial Decline in Britain since 1900* (1988) and Perry Anderson, 'The Figures of Descent', *New Left Review*, 161 (Jan–Feb 1987), present a broader picture. See also the responses to Anderson in subsequent issues of the *New Left Review* by Michael Barratt Brown, Alex Callinicos and David Edgerton (1991). E. P. Thompson's 1965 essay criticizing Anderson and Nairn, 'The Peculiarities of the English', in *The Poverty of Theory* (1978), should be read by all tempted by the declinist thesis since it brilliantly exposes the use of fairy-story histories of Other Countries in analyses of England. R. J. Collingwood's account in his *The Idea of History* (Oxford, 1946) of the idiocies of popular histories of English progress, and their relation to academic history, will protect readers from the modern English disease of inverted Whiggism. The account, in his *An Autobiography* (Oxford, 1939), of the astonishing blindness of academics who prided themselves on their realism will also help. See also Sidney Pollard's *Britain's Prime and Britain's Decline* (1989) (though not his *The Wasting of the British Economy* (1982)) and Donald McCloskey's *Econometric History* (1987).

It is not uncommon to find the argument that failures in science and technology were an important cause of the economic 'decline', even though it is very difficult to find a convincing one. Nevertheless it is to be found in D. S. L. Cardwell, *The Organisation of Science in England* (1957, 1972), H. Rose and S. Rose, *Science and Society* (Harmondsworth, 1969), K. Pavitt (ed.), *Technical Innovation and British Economic Performance* (1980) and Correlli Barnett, *The Audit of War* (1986). In most of these works there is a failure to analyse adequately the actual relations between science and technology and economic growth, to make proper international comparisons or to describe fully the sources of funding for science and technology. Thus warnings, even from a figure like David Landes in *The Unbound Prometheus* (1969), that for many countries after the Second World War there was no correlation between civil R & D spending and economic growth have been ignored. Biased and incomplete international comparisons of English support of R & D with that of selected other countries continue to be made; let us hope that Sidney Pollard's excellent comparison of English and German support of science and technology before 1914, in *Britain's Prime and Britain's Decline* (1989) will be noted. Let us hope too that the fact that in the early 1960s British industry spent more on R & D than any industry of the other OECD countries except the US (see *OECD International Statistical Year for Research and Development: A Study of the Resources devoted to R & D in OECD Member Countries in 1963/64*, 2 vols (Paris, 1968), will be remembered. The last problem is that most of the literature on English science and technology in the twentieth century concentrates on state-funded civil research and development without recognizing that state-funded defence and industry-funded civil R & D were both considerably larger for most of this century. This bias vitiates many of the arguments of standard works like Cardwell, *Organization of Science* or Rose and Rose, *Science and Society* (for the pre-1945 period). It means that works like N. Vig, *Science and Technology in British Politics* (Oxford, 1968) and P. G. Gummett, *Scientists in Whitehall* (Manchester, 1980) should be read carefully since they are concerned only with the state-funded civil side. A better-balanced picture for the pre-1945 period can be obtained from reading Michael Sanderson, 'Research and the Firm in British Industry, 1919–39', *Science Studies*, 2 (1972), pp. 107–51, and D. E. H. Edgerton, 'Science and Technology in British Business History', *Business History*, 29 (1987), pp. 84–103.

War, Economy and Ideology

The 'war and society' literature may be divided into two sorts. The first is the work of conservative military historians. Two elegant examples of the genre are Michael Howard, *War in European History* (Oxford, 1976) and Brian Bond, *War and Society in Europe, 1870–1970* (1984). The second is a social democratic literature on societies at war, concentrating on the social and political history of the 'home front'. Excellent examples are Arthur Marwick, *Britain in the Century of Total War* (1968); Paul Addison, *The Road to 1945* (1975); and Angus Calder, *The People's War* (1969) – the preface to the 1976 edition suggests the author would now place a question mark after the title. The traditional account stressing social benefits from war is criticized in Harold L. Smith (ed.), *War and Social Change: British Society in the Second World War* (Manchester, 1986). The 'new sociology of war' has produced a great deal of interesting work in recent years, e.g. Martin Shaw, *The Dialectics of War and Peace* (1988); Martin Shaw (ed.), *War, State and Society* (1984); Colin Creighton and Martin Shaw (eds.), *The Sociology of War and Peace* (1987); Anthony Giddens, *The Nation State and Violence* (1985). See also *New Left Review* (eds.), *Exterminism and Cold War* (1982). Other interesting new directions are studies of the relations of ideology and economics to strategy. Paul Kennedy has written a number of books on economics and strategy, for example, *The Realities Behind Diplomacy: Background Influences on British External Policy, 1986–1980* (1981), *Strategy and Diplomacy, 1870–1945: Eight Studies* (1983), *The Rise and Fall of the Great Powers: Economic Change and Military Conflict from 1500–2000* (1988). David French, *British Economic and Strategic Planning, 1905–1915* (1982) and G. C. Peden, *British Rearmament and the Treasury 1932–1939* (Edinburgh, 1979) are also indispensable. Much of this literature assumes British defence expenditure was low in the 1920s and early 1930s, an argument debunked by John Ferris in 'Treasury Control: The Ten Year Rule and British Service Policies, 1919–1924', *Historical Journal*, 30 (1987), pp. 859–83. The equally common assumption that the armaments industry was weak and technically backward is challenged in David Edgerton, 'Liberal Militarism and the British State', *New Left Review*, 185 (1991), pp. 138–69, and G. A. H. Gordon, *British Seapower and Procurement between the Wars: A Reappraisal of Rearmament* (1988). The relations between British politics and ideology and the nature of Britain's mode of warfare is not much explored, but there are some excellent works available. Michael Howard, *War and the Liberal Conscience* (Oxford, 1981) is brief and very useful; Bernard Semmel, *Liberalism and Naval Strategy: Ideology, Interest and Sea Power during the Pax Britannica* (1986) is a brilliant work. Hew Strachan, 'The British Way in Warfare Revisited', *Historical Journal*, 26 (1983), pp. 447–61, challenges the conventional military-historical approach to defence history, stressing the importance of the Navy and the Air Force. Many studies now exist on peace movements. James Hinton, *Protests and Visions: Peace Politics in Twentieth Century Britain* (1989) is the best way into this literature. Anti-liberal thinkers are much less well-served, but useful and interesting studies of the Edwardian years in particular may be found in Paul Kennedy (ed.), *Nationalist and Racialist Movements in Britain and Germany before 1914* (1981), A. J. A. Morris, *The Scaremongers: The Advocacy of War and Rearmament, 1896–1914* (1984) and J. H. Grainger, *Patriotisms: Britain 1900–1939* (1986). It is difficult to suggest works on the attitude of the right to defence thereafter. It is interesting to note, for example, that such perceptive general works on militarism as Volker Berghahn, *Militarism: The History of an International Debate, 1861–1979* (Cambridge, 1984) and Martin Ceadel, *Thinking about War and Peace* (Oxford, 1986) have very little to say on the specific nature of English militarism. Ian Beckett and John Gooch (eds.), *Politicians and Defence: Studies in the Formulation of British Defence Policy,*

1845–1970 (Manchester, 1981), deals mainly with the Army, but contains useful essays on Duncan Sandys and Denis Healey.

The Royal Air Force

The history of the RAF has been neglected by comparison with the Army. In recent years, however, many good works have appeared. Malcolm Cooper, *The Birth of Independent Air Power* (1986) is the best source on the First World War. W. J. Reader, *Architect of Air Power: The Life of the First Viscount Weir of Eastwood, 1877–1959* (1968) is a good biography of Weir covering his role in the First World War and the 1930s. Barry D. Powers, *Strategy without Slide-Rule: British Air Strategy, 1914–1939* (1976) contains many examples of the exaggerated fear of the bomber, a theme explored in detail for the 1930s in Uri Bialer, *The Shadow of the Bomber: The Fear of Air Attack and British Politics, 1932–1939* (1980). The best overall study of the RAF in the interwar years is Malcolm Smith, *British Air Strategy Between the Wars* (Oxford, 1984). H. M. Hyde, *British Air Policy Between the Wars, 1918–1939* (1976) should be read knowing that the author was Lord Londonderry's secretary in the 1930s. The anti-French expansion of the RAF in the 1920s is discussed in John Ferris, 'The Theory of a "French Air Menace": Anglo-French Relations and the British Home Defence Air Force Programmes of 1921–25', *Journal of Strategic Studies*, 10 (1987), pp. 62–83. The best way into 'air control' in the Empire is Charles Townshend, *Britain's Civil Wars* (1986) since, as the title suggests, it is put in context. Jafna L. Cox, 'A Splendid Training Ground: The Importance to the RAF of its role in Iraq, 1919–1932', *Journal of Imperial and Commonwealth History*, 13 (1985), pp. 157–84, gives details. Air Vice-Marshal A. G. Dudgeon's entertaining and informative memoir, *The Luck of the Devil: An Autobiography, 1934–*

1941 (Shrewsbury, 1985) is particularly good on the lifestyle of RAF officers and on 'air control' on the North-West Frontier. G. C. Peden, 'The Burden of Imperial Defence and the Continental Commitment Reconsidered', *Historical Journal*, 27 (1984), pp. 405–23, shows clearly that the thesis that imperial defence damaged home defence in the 1930s is wrong. The literature on the RAF in the Second World War is vast. The best comparative account is R. J. Overy, *The Air War 1939–1945* (1980). The broadest in scope and analysis is John Terraine's fine *The Right of the Line: The Royal Air Force in the European War, 1939–1945* (1985). More damning detail on bombing may be found in C. Webster and N. Frankland, *The Strategic Air Offensive against Germany, 1939–1945*, 4 vols (1961). The sheer scale of Bomber Command's operations may be readily appreciated by consulting Martin Middlebrook and Chris Everrit, *The Bomber Command War Diaries: An Operational Reference Book, 1939–1945* (1985) and Martin Middlebrook, *The Nuremberg Raid, 30–31 March 1943* (1973). For the naval origins of strategic bombing, see N. Frankland, *The Bombing Offensive against Germany* (1965) and N. Jones, *The Origins of Strategic Bombing* (1973). For the wartime opposition to the 'night bombing' of Germany see Vera Brittain, *Testament of a Peace Lover: Letters from Vera Brittain*, edited by Winifred and Alan Eden-Green (1988). *The Proceedings of the Royal Air Force Historical Society* are particularly useful for the post-war years.

Science, Technology and War

The relations of science, technology, industry and war is a tricky area: D. E. H. Edgerton briefly explains why in 'Science and War' in R. C. Olby et al. (eds.), *The Companion to the History of Modern Science* (1990), and gives an equally brief account of the idea of 'spin-off' in 'The Relationship between Military and Civil Technologies:

A Historical Perspective', in P. J. Gummet and J. Reppy, *The Relations between Defence and Civil Technologies* (Dordrecht, 1988). There are now a number of good full-length books on technology and war: for example, Mary Kaldor, *The Baroque Arsenal* (1982); W. H. McNeill, *The Pursuit of Power: Technology, Armed Force and Society since AD 1000* (Oxford, 1983), which is best up to 1914; Maurice Pearton, *The Knowledgeable State: Diplomacy, War and Technology since 1830* (1982); J. M. Winter (ed.), *War and Economic Development* (Cambridge, 1975); Guy Hartcup, *The War of Invention: Scientific Developments 1914–1918* (1988) and *The Challenge of War: Scientific and Engineering Contributions to World War Two* (Newton Abbot, 1970). However, most of these works assume that science, technology and industry are essentially civil phenomena which impinge on the armed services and war from the outside. For a different emphasis see the paper by David Noble in Merrit Roe Smith (ed.), *Military Enterprise and Technological Change: Perspectives on the American Experience* (Cambridge, Mass., 1985); B. C. Hacker and S. L. Hacker, 'Military Institutions and the Labour Process: Non-Economic Sources of Technological Change, Women's Subordination and the Organization of Work', *Technology and Culture*, 28 (1987), pp. 743–75; Paul Forman, 'Behind Quantum Electronics', *Historical Studies in the Physical and Biological Sciences*, 18, Part I (1987), pp. 149–229.

The Aircraft Industry to 1945

The quantity of material on particular aircraft is quite extraordinary. It is itself an index of the enthusiasm aeroplanes have generated that loving compilations, full of the most extraordinary detail, have been produced of practically every type of aeroplane ever made in Britain; for some aeroplane types every individual copy has been traced. By far the most comprehensive series of books is that published by Putnam. The following is a partial list: C. H. Barnes, *Bristol Aircraft since 1910* (1964); C. H. Barnes, *Shorts' Aircraft since 1900* (1967); A. J. Jackson, *Blackburn Aircraft since 1909* (1968); D. N. James, *Gloster Aircraft since 1917* (1971); F. K. Mason, *Hawker Aircraft since 1920*, 2nd edn (1971). New editions of many have been published. C. F. Andrews and E. B. Morgan, *Supermarine Aircraft since 1914* (1981, 1987) is typical of this genre in that it confines itself largely to the technical aspects of each aeroplane produced: it notes Pemberton Billing's notoriety and Lady Houston's hatred of the Labour Party without giving any of the essential details. Enthusiasts also have their own magazines, notably *Aeroplane Monthly* and *Flypast.* Harald Penrose's multi-volume *British Aviation* (1967–80), which covers the period from the beginning to 1939 is, while very useful as a source, little more than compacted cuttings from *The Aeroplane* punctuated by royal and RAF events. The most useful sources for the industry to the end of the First World War are R. Dallas Brett, *A History of British Aviation 1908–1914* (1934, re-issued 1988) and H. A. Jones, *The War in the Air*, vol. 3 (Oxford, 1931), which remains the best source for the Great War also. Percy Walker's history of *Early Aviation at Farnborough*, 2 vols (1971, 1974), is very biased towards Farnborough and against the private manufacturers. The interwar years are much better served, notably by the articles of Peter Fearon: 'The Formative Years of the British Aircraft Industry, 1913–1924', *Business History Review*, 43 (1969), pp. 476–95; 'The Vicissitudes of a British Aircraft Company: Handley Page Limited between the Wars', *Business History*, 20 (1978), pp. 63–86; 'The British Airframe Industry and the State, 1918–35', *Economic History Review*, 27 (1974), pp. 236–51; 'Aircraft Manufacturing', in N. K. Buxton and D. H. Aldcroft (eds.), *British Industry between the Wars* (1979), pp. 216–40. Alec Robertson made some important points defending the British industry in 'The British Airframe Industry and the State in the Interwar Period: A Comment',

Economic History Review, 28 (1975), pp. 648–57, to which Fearon replied in 'The British Airframe Industry and the State in the Interwar Period: A Reply', *Economic History Review*, 28 (1975), pp. 658–62. Malcolm Smith, *British Air Strategy between the Wars* (Oxford, 1984) has some new material on 1930s aircraft production. See also the entries for the aircraft industry in D. J. Jeremy (ed.), *Dictionary of Business Biography*, 5 vols (1984–6). The most useful contemporary sources are the pages of *The Aeroplane* and R. McKinnon Wood, *Aircraft Manufacture: A Description of the Industry and Proposal for its Socialisation* (New Fabian Research Bureau, 1935), *Minutes of Evidence* and *Report of the Royal Commission on the Private Manufacture of and Trading in Arms* 1935, 36, Cmd. 5292, *PP* 1935/36 vol. vii, as well as the *Statement Relating to the Report of the Royal Commission on the Private Manufacture of and Trading in Arms* 1935, 36, Cmd. 5451, *PP* 1936/37 vol. xxi. On trade in aircraft, see Anthony Sampson, *The Arms Bazaar: The Companies, the Dealers, the Bribes: From Vickers to Lockheed* (1977), and John Ferris, 'A British "Unofficial" Aviation Mission and Japanese Naval Developments, 1919–1929', *Journal of Strategic Studies*, 5 (1982), pp. 416–39. On the SBAC in the 1930s and much else, see R. P. Shay, *British Rearmament in the Thirties: Politics and Profits* (Princeton, 1977). For the period of rearmament and war, the most complete treatment is still to be found in the official histories of war production. M. M. Postan, *British War Production* (1952) introduces the series of which the most relevant to aircraft production are W. Ashworth, *Contracts and Finance* (1953), M. M. Postan, D. Hay and J. D. Scott, *Design and Development of Weapons* (1964), J. D. Scott and R. Hughes, *The Administration of War Production* (1955) and W. Hornby, *Factories and Plant* (1958). The Ministry of Aircraft Production's pamphlet, written by the novelist Nigel Balchin, *The Aircraft Builders: An Account of British Aircraft Production, 1935–45* (1947) is a useful brief account. On some issues the official histories can mislead: for an example, see D. E. H. Edgerton, 'Technical Innovation, Industrial Capacity and Efficiency: Public Ownership and the British Military Aircraft Industry, 1935–1948', *Business History*, 26 (1984), pp. 247–79. Eric Mensforth, a senior figure in the Ministry, wrote a useful overview of production, 'Airframe Production', *Aircraft Production*, 9 (1947), pp. 343–50, 388–95, which may be supplemented with his autobiography, *Family Engineers* (1981). The production of aircraft in the Second World War is surprisingly little studied. The best source is R. J. Overy, *The Air War, 1939–1945* (1980). A. Henshaw, *The Sigh of the Merlin* (1979) is a useful memoir which contains much information about the Castle Bromwich Spitfire plant. The labour aspects of aircraft production are dealt with in many works concerning wartime work: the official history by P. Inman, *Labour in the Munitions Industries* (1957), J. B. Jefferys, *The Story of the Engineers* (1945) and Richard Croucher, *The Engineers at War, 1939–1945* (1982). For the Ministry of Aircraft Production the best sources are the official history, *Administration of War Production*, and D. E. H. Edgerton, 'State Intervention in British Manufacturing Industry, 1931–1951: A Comparison of Policy for the Military Aircraft and Cotton Textile Industries', Ph.D. thesis (University of London, 1986): my discussion of state–aircraft industry relations in Chapters 2, 4 and 5 draws on this. See also my 'The Ministry of Supply, the Aircraft Industry and Defence R & D' in Helen Mercer et al. (eds.), *The 1945 Labour Government and the Private Sector* (Edinburgh, 1992). A. J. P. Taylor's hagiographical *Beaverbrook* (1972) should be read in conjunction with A. J. Robertson, 'Lord Beaverbrook and the Supply of Aircraft, 1940–1941', in A. Slaven and D. H. Aldcroft (eds.), *Business, Banking and Urban History: Essays in Honour of S. G. Checkland* (Edinburgh, 1982), which shows that the increase in supply of aircraft in 1940 owed little to Beaverbrook. The most useful memoir is F. R. (Rod) Banks, *I Kept No Diary* (Shrewsbury, 1978): the author held various senior posts dealing with engine production. Unfortunately, neither of the two biographies of Stafford Cripps deal adequately with his period at MAP: C. A. Cooke, *The Life of Richard Stafford Cripps* (1957); E. Estorick, *Stafford Cripps: A Biography* (1949). Angus Calder, *The People's War* (1969) is good on Cripps and some of the failures of wartime planning. A MAP official, Ely Devons, wrote a classic on planning in general in *Planning in Practice: Essays in Aircraft Planning in Wartime* (Cambridge, 1950). The big armourers' involvement in aircraft production is covered in J. D. Scott, *Vickers: A History* (1962), which does not tell the full story of Noel Pemberton Billing, and M. S. Moss and J. R. Hume, *Beardmore: The History of a Scottish Industrial Giant* (1979). As in the case of the RAF, there will doubtless be many books published on the aircraft industry in the coming years. Peter King's *Knights of the Air* (1989), despite the cliché title, provides a good overview of the main aircraft firms from the beginning into the post-war years.

Technical Development

No treatment of state funding of science and technology gives adequate consideration to research supported by the services, and thus to aeronautical R & D. The best studies of the development of aircraft technology are R. Miller and D. Sawers, *The Technical Development of Modern Aviation* (1968), which, despite its title, deals only with civil aircraft, and R. Schlaifer and R. D. Heron, *The Development of Aircraft Engines and Aviation Fuels* (Boston, Mass., 1950). E. Constant, *The Turbojet Revolution* (Baltimore, 1980), provides the best introduction to the development of aerodynamics until 1945, as well as the best account of the multiple invention of the jet engine. C. H. Gibbs-Smith, *Aviation: An Historical Survey from its Origins to the End of World War II* (1970) is really a study of technical development, as is the older M. J. B. Davy, *Interpretive History of Flight*, 2nd edn (1948).

The organization of aeronautical R & D is difficult to piece together: there was no official history of science and technology written beyond M. M. Postan, D. Hay and J. D. Scott, *Design and Development of Weapons* (1964) which contains useful information, as does J. D. Scott and R. Hughes, *The Administration of War Production* (1955). The official *Fifty Years at Farnborough* (1955) may be supplemented with the Earl of Birkenhead, *The Prof in Two Worlds* (1961), a biography of Lord Cherwell, who as Frederick Lindemann, worked at Farnborough in the First World War. *The Prof in Two Worlds* also disposes of C. P. Snow's typically wrongheaded account of the Tizard–Cherwell dispute over strategic bombing in the Second World War. See also M. J. Lighthill, 'The Royal Aircraft Establishment', in Sir John Cockcroft (ed.), *The Organisation of Research Establishments* (1966). Michael Sanderson's *The Universities and British Industry 1859–1970* (1972) contains much information on aeronautics in universities. T. J. N. Hilken, *Engineering at Cambridge, 1783–1965* (Cambridge, 1967) covers Cambridge. Since many of the important aeronautical engineers were elected Fellows of the Royal Society, the annual *Biographical Memoirs of Fellows of the Royal Society* provides a convenient and very useful source. The journal *Technology and Culture* should be consulted for recent, and largely American, work on the development of aviation: for example, R. K. Smith, 'The Intercontinental Airliner and the Essence of Airplane Performance, 1929–1939', *Technology and Culture*, 24 (1983), an article which shows that some conventional measures of performance are misleading and that flying boats were not a dead end. See also I. B. Holley, 'A Detroit Dream of Mass-produced Fighter Aircraft: The XP-75 Fiasco', *Technology and Culture*, 28 (1987), pp. 578–93. As befits their popularity, many of the leading engineers and pioneers have been the subjects of biographies or have written their autobiographies, for example R. W. Clark, *Tizard* (1965); Sir Stanley Hooker, assisted by Bill Gunston, *Not Much of an Engineer: An Autobiography*

(Shrewsbury, 1984); Sir Frank Whittle, *Jet: The Story of a Pioneer* (1953); John Golley, *Whittle: The True Story* (Shrewsbury, 1987); Geoffrey de Havilland, *Sky Fever: The Autobiography of Sir Geoffrey de Havilland* (1961); Bill Gunston, *By Jupiter! The Life of Sir Roy Fedden* (1978); J. E. Morpurgo, *Barnes Wallis: A Biography* (1972); Nevil Shute, *Slide Rule* (1954).

Aviation and British Culture

Technological enthusiasm has been assumed to be absent from English culture in the twentieth century. The reasons for this are very complex, but much of the blame can be laid on C. P. Snow's *The Two Cultures and the Scientific Revolution* (Cambridge, 1959). Snow's crude and misleading analysis is, however, an excellent example of technological enthusiasm, and its very great impact should in part be taken as a measure of that enthusiasm in English culture. Much the same might be said of the equally wrongheaded and fundamentally similar account in Martin Wiener, *English Culture and the Decline of the Industrial Spirit, 1850–1980* (Cambridge, 1981). For a rebuttal, see Michael Sanderson, 'The English Civic Universities and the "Industrial Spirit", 1870–1914', *Historical Research*, 61 (1988), pp. 90–104. A rare study of technological enthusiasm in Britain is Bill Luckin, *Questions of Power: Electricity and Environment in Inter-War Britain* (Manchester, 1990). The importance of literary enthusiasm for technology in England may be traced in Norman and Jeanne MacKensie, *H. G. Wells: A Biography* (New York, 1973) and I. F. Clarke, *The Pattern of Expectation, 1644–2001* (1979). Books that cover technological enthusiasm in general are Langdon Winner, *Autonomous Technology: Technics-out-of-Control as a Theme in Political Thought* (Cambridge, Mass., 1977), and Stephen Kern, *The Culture of Time and Space, 1880–1918* (1983). But we need English analogues of Jeffrey Herf, *Reactionary Modernism: Technology, Culture and Politics in Weimar and the Third Reich* (Cambridge, 1985), David Noble, *America by Design: Science, Technology and the Rise of Corporate Capitalism* (New York, 1977) and Thomas P. Hughes, *American Genesis: A Century of Invention and Technological Enthusiasm* (New York, 1989). English aviation did not produce a Saint-Exupéry, but many writers were fascinated by aviation, as is catalogued in Valentine Cunningham, *British Writers of the Thirties* (Oxford, 1988). Gillian Beer deals with a particularly interesting example in 'The Island and the Aeroplane: The Case of Virginia Woolf' in Homi K. Bhabha (ed.), *Nation and Narration* (1990). Perhaps the most important works are H. G. Wells, *The Shape of Things to Come: The Ultimate Revolution* (1933); T. E. Lawrence, *The Mint* (1955, unexpurgated edition reissued 1988); and Rex Warner, *The Aerodrome: A Love Story* (1941, 1982). Very interesting commentaries on Wells and Lawrence may be found in Christopher Caudwell, *Studies in a Dying Culture* (1938). George Orwell's wartime criticism of Wells, 'Wells, Hitler and the World State', *The Collected Essays, Journalism and Letters of George Orwell*, vol. II (1968), is very important. *Men of the RAF* (1942) contains drawings of RAF personnel made by Sir William Rothenstein, as well as revealing essays by him and by Lord David Cecil. Paul Nash, *Outline: An Autobiography and Other Essays* (1949) contains 'The Personality of Planes', published in *Vogue*, March 1942. Two American works, Paul Fussell, *Wartime: Understanding and Behaviour in the Second World War* (1989) and Thomas Pynchon, *Gravity's Rainbow* (1973) should be consulted to see what English writers might have but have not written. On Pynchon and technology, see Joseph W. Slade, 'Thomas Pynchon, Postindustrial Humanist', *Technology and Culture*, 23 (1982), pp. 53–72. See also Dale Carter, *The Final Frontier: The Rise and Fall of the American Rocket State* (1988). The relations of aviation and the cinema have not had the attention they deserve. Paul Virilio's *War and Cinema: The Logistics of Perception*, trans. Patrick Camiller (1989), is suggestive. There is now a substantial literature on British cinema in the Second World War, for example Philip M. Taylor (ed.), *Britain and the Cinema in the Second World War* (1988) and Michael Powell's autobiography, *A Life in Movies* (1986), but I know of nothing on the aviation films. English air-mindedness has not been treated in detail, but the best sources are Uri Bialer, *The Shadow of the Bomber: The Fear of Air Attack and British Politics 1932–1939* (1980) and Barry D. Powers, *Strategy without Slide-Rule: British Air Strategy, 1914–1939* (1976). The social connotations are clear in Mary S. Lovell, *Straight On Till Morning: The Life of Beryl Markham* (1987) and A. Henshaw, *The Sigh of the Merlin* (1979). The American version of air-mindedness is covered in Joseph Corn, *The Winged Gospel: America's Romance with Aviation, 1900–1950* (New York, 1984), though the essentially liberal basis of American air-mindedness is not pointed out. Corn is usefully supplemented by Gore Vidal's essay 'On Flying', in *Armageddon? Essays 1983–1987* (1987). The Soviet case is covered in K. E. Bailes, 'Technology and Legitimacy: Society, Aviation and Stalinism in the 1930's', *Technology and Culture*, 17 (1976), pp. 55–81; the German in George L. Mosse, 'War and the Appropriation of Nature', in V. R. Berghahn and Martin Kitchen (eds.), *Germany in the Age of Total War: Essays in Honour of Francis Carsten* (1981); the French in Robert Wohl, 'Par la voie des airs: l'entrée de l'aviation dans le monde de lettres françaises, 1909–1939', *Le Mouvement Social*, 145 (1988), pp. 41–64; and the Italian in *Futurism in Flight: 'Aeropittura' Paintings and Sculptures of Man's Conquest of Space (1913–1945)* (1990). On airline pilots, see A. N. Blain, *Pilots and Management: Industrial Relations in the UK Airlines* (1972).

Politics

Easily the best book on the early politics of the aeroplane is Alfred Gollin, *No Longer an Island: Britain and the Wright Brothers, 1902–*

1909 (1984). Chapter 1 is much indebted to this fine book. The importance of Pemberton Billing was noted by A. J. P. Taylor in his *English History, 1914–1945* (Oxford, 1965); further details may be found in Barry D. Powers, *Strategy without Slide-Rule* (1976), and details of the famous libel action in G. R. Searle, *Corruption in British Politics, 1895–1930* (Oxford, 1987). See also, Noel Pemberton Billing's own *P-B: The Story of his Life* (Hertford: The Imperialist Press, 1917). More generally on aeronautical politics in the First World War, see Malcolm Cooper, *The Birth of Independent Air Power* (1986). For the importance of imperialism in the interwar years, see John M. MacKensie (ed.), *Imperialism and Popular Culture* (Manchester, 1986). For the attitudes of writers towards armaments, see Ivan Melada, *Guns for Sale: War and Capitalism in English Literature, 1851–1939* (Jefferson, North Carolina, 1983). Richard Griffiths, *Fellow Travellers of the Right: British Enthusiasts for Nazi Germany, 1933–39* (1980) is of vital importance to the study of the atmosphere of the 1930s. Lady Houston, Lord Sempill, Sir Arnold Wilson, Lord Londonderry, Lord Rothermere, Admiral Sueter and C. G. Grey all figure prominently, though not all are linked to aviation or science. Robert Skidelsky, *Oswald Mosley* (1975) is also indispensable. Some biographies and autobiographies which are useful are J. A. Cross, *Lord Swinton* (Oxford, 1982) and *Sir Samuel Hoare: A Political Biography* (1977), Viscount Swinton, *I Remember* (1948), Viscount Rothermere, *My Fight to Rearm Britain* (1939). The politics of scientists and engineers is a topic which is barely explored. See Frank M. Turner, 'Public Science in Britain, 1880–1919', *Isis*, 71 (1980), pp. 589–608. For the interwar scientific left, see P. G. Werskey, *The Visible College* (1978, 1988) which provides a vivid contrast to the usual picture of the interwar intellectual left as arty members of the 'Homintern'. Still missing is an account of the scientific right. Sir Arnold Wilson figures, though not his politics, in W. H. G. Armytage, *Sir Richard Gregory: His Life and Work* (1957), the biography of the editor of *Nature*, a leading advocate for science and close friend of H. G. Wells.

Post-War Aviation

On the Labour Party, see Ralph Miliband, *Parliamentary Socialism*, 2nd edn (1972). Memoirs and diaries are a useful source for aviation and defence in the 1960s, notably Denis Healey, *The Time of My Life* (1989), Tony Benn, *Out of the Wilderness: Diaries 1963–1967* (1987) and *Office Without Power: Diaries 1968–1972* (1988), and Solly Zuckerman, *Monkeys, Men and Missiles* (1988). Two rare treatments of post-war defence R & D are Council for Science and Society, *UK Military R & D: Report of a Working Party* (Oxford, 1986) and P. J. Gummett, 'Defence Research Policy', in M. Goldsmith (ed.), *UK Science Policy: A Critical Review of Policies for Publicly-funded Research* (Harlow, 1984). Standard works on industrial policy and the development of the state machine like S. Young with A. V. Lowe, *Intervention in the Mixed Economy: The Evolution of Industrial Policy, 1964–1972* (1974) ignore defence. As has been noted, the supply ministries are unknown to most historians. An excellent summary of their history to 1964 may be found in D. N. Chester and F. M. G. Willson, *The Organisation of British Central Government, 1914–1964*, 2nd edn (1968). F. M. G. Willson is one of the few people to have got the story of Mintech straight: see his 'Coping with Administrative Growth: Super-departments and the Ministerial Cadre, 1957–1977', in D. Butler and A. H. Halsey (eds.), *Policy and Politics: Essays in Honour of Norman Chester* (1978). The best short account of the ambitions of Mintech was given by Tony Benn in a lecture at the Imperial College of Science and Technology, *The Government's Policy for Technology* (1967). For the origins of Mintech, see Harold Wilson, 'The State and Private Industry' (1950), Public Record Office, PREM8/1183; A. Jones, *Britain's Economy: The Roots of Stagnation* (Cambridge, 1985); Harold Wilson,

The Relevance of British Socialism (1964) and my 'Liberal Militarism and the British State', *New Left Review*, 135 (1991), pp. 138–69. For the post-war aircraft industry, see K. Hayward, *Government and British Civil Aerospace: A Case Study in Post-war Technology Policy* (Manchester, 1983), and *The British Aircraft Industry* (Manchester, 1989). No aircraft firm has an adequate business history, with the possible exception of BAC, covered by Charles Gardner in *BAC: A History* (1981), which is a good source for the post-war industry as a whole. See also Harold Evans, *Vickers Against the Odds, 1956–1977* (1978); W. J. Baker, *A History of the Marconi Company* (1970) – a firm owned by English Electric from 1946, on which see R. Jones and O. Marriott, *Anatomy of a Merger: The History of GEC, AEI and English Electric* (1970). Very useful accounts and analyses of shorter periods may be found in Ely Devons, 'The Aircraft Industry' in Duncan Burn (ed.), *The Structure of British Industry*, vol. 2 (Cambridge, 1958), *Supply of Military Aircraft*, Cmd. 9388, *PP* 1954/55, vol. xi, and above all in *Report of the Committee of Inquiry into the Aircraft Industry*, Cmd. 2853 (1965) [Plowden Report]. On the TSR2, see G. Williams, F. Gregory and J. Simpson, *Crisis in Procurement: A Case Study of the TSR2* (1970). There is a whole series of Concorde books: an example is Andrew Wilson, *The Concorde Fiasco* (1973). A. Reed, *Britain's Aircraft Industry: What went Right? What went Wrong?* (1973) and D. Wood, *Project Cancelled* (1975) are two useful polemical works. David Henderson's 1985 Reith Lectures published as *Innocence and Design* (1986) are a neo-liberal critique of what he calls Do-It-Yourself-Economics, essentially naive technocratic enthusiasm for technology and manufacturing.

Subsequent Literature

The years since 1990 have seen an explosion in literature on the subjects of this book. What was barely addressed in 1990 is now the subject of many books; the interpretations prevalent in 1990 now seem, in many cases, quaintly outdated. That said, *England and the Aeroplane* fits into the new literature much better than it did with what was around when it was written.

The question of national identity increased in significance for historians of twentieth-century Britain, with much attention given to the Second World War and Empire. Raphael Samuel, *Theatres of Memory*, vol. II, *Island Stories* (1998); Robert Colls, *Identity of England* (Oxford, 2002); Richard Weight, *Patriots: National Identity in Britain 1940–2000* (2002); Wendy Webster, *Englishness and Empire 1939–1965* (Oxford, 2005); and in a different vein, Peter Mandler, *The English National Character: The History of an Idea from Edmund Burke to Tony Blair* (2006). Anthony Barnett, *Iron Britannia* (1982) has been republished with an extensive new introduction as *Iron Britannia: Time to Take the Great out of Britain* (2012).

The question of decline remained important into the late 1990s. Among the most interesting contributions were David Coates, *The Question of UK Decline: The Economy, State and Society* (1994); Andrew Cox, Simon Lee, and Joe Sanderson, *The Political Economy Of Modern Britain* (1997); Richard English and Michael Kenny (eds.) *Rethinking British Decline* (1999); and Peter Clarke and Clive Trebilcock (eds.), *Understanding Decline: Perceptions and Realities of British Economic Performance* (Cambridge, 1997). Some of this work took *England and the Aeroplane* to be discussing a phenomenon that itself contributed to decline, an argument most extensively advanced in Maurice Kirby, 'British Culture and the Development of High Technology Sectors', in Andrew Godley and Oliver M. Westall (eds.), *Business History and Business Culture* (Manchester, 1996). On the nature of the British business class, see Martin Daunton, '"Gentlemanly Capitalism" and British Industry, 1820–1914', *Past and Present*, 122, (1989), pp. 119–58, and the exchange with W. D. Rubinstein in *Past & Present*, 132 (1991), pp. 150–70, 170–87. W. D. Rubinstein,

Capitalism, Culture and Decline in Britain, 1750–1990 (1993) should be read in that context and in the light of F. M. L. Thompson, *Gentrification and the Enterprise Culture: Britain 1780–1980* (Oxford, 1993). The modernity of British business has been emphasized in many articles by Leslie Hannah.

Things have changed so much that George Bernstein has a book called *The Myth of Decline: The Rise of Britain since 1945* (2004). Decline is now definitely passé, and declinism has become a term of art. For a discussion of its meanings, see my 'The Prophet Militant and Industrial: The Peculiarities of Correlli Barnett', *Twentieth Century British History*, 2 (1991), pp. 360–79, and *Science, Technology and the British Industrial 'Decline'* (Cambridge, 1996); Jim Tomlinson, *The Politics of Decline: Understanding Post-war Britain* (2000), and his essays on the topic, starting with 'Inventing "Decline": The Falling Behind of the British Economy in the Postwar Years', *Economic History Review*, 49 (1996), pp. 731–57; and Guy Ortolano, *The Two Cultures Controversy: Science, Literature, and Cultural Politics in Postwar Britain* (Cambridge, 2009). For a post-declinist economic history, see for example, Alan Booth, *The British Economy in the Twentieth Century* (2001).

Declinist assumptions were influential in cultural history and studies of national identity long after they ceased to be convincing in economic history. Yet there were counter-arguments here too. Alison Light, *Forever England: Femininity, Literature and Conservatism Between the Wars* (1991) looks at the conservative embrace of modernity. A new sensibility about Britain and modernity is obvious in Peter Mandler, 'Against "Englishness": English Culture and the Limits to Rural Nostalgia, 1850–1940', *Transactions of the Royal Historical Society* (Sixth Series), 7 (1997), pp. 155–75; David Matless, *Landscape and Englishness* (1998); Becky Conekin, Frank Mort and Chris Water, *Moments of Modernity: Reconstructing Britain, 1945–1964* (1999); Martin Daunton and Bernhard Rieger (eds.), *Meanings of Modernity: Britain from the Late Victorian Era to World War II* (2001); and in Alexandra Harris, *Romantic Moderns: English Writers, Artists and the Imagination from Virginia Woolf to John Piper* (2010). Aviation is central in a series of rich new cultural histories, such as Ian Patterson, *Guernica and Total War* (2007), Peter Deer, *Culture in Camouflage: War, Empire, and Modern British Literature* (Oxford, 2009), Leo Mellor, *Reading the Ruins: Modernism, Bombsites and British Culture* (Cambridge, 2011) and Susan R. Grayzel, *At Home and Under Fire: Air Raids and Culture in Britain from the Great War to the Blitz* (Cambridge, 2011).

The modernity of Empire has been stressed by among others Peder Anker, *Imperial Ecology: Environmental Order in the British Empire, 1895–1945* (Cambridge, Mass., 2001) and Sabine Clarke, 'A Technocratic Imperial State? The Colonial Office and Scientific Research, 1940–1960', *Twentieth Century British History*, 18 (2007), pp. 453–80; Joseph Hodge, *Triumph of the Expert: Agrarian Doctrines of Development and the Legacies of British Colonialism* (Athens, Ohio, 2007); Helen Tilley, *Africa as a Living Laboratory: Empire, Development, and the Problem of Scientific Knowledge* (Chicago, 2011). Empire and aviation has attracted a good deal of attention, for example Liz Millward, *Women in British Imperial Airspace, 1922–1937* (Montreal, 2007); Priya Satia, 'The Defense of Inhumanity: Air Control in Iraq and the British Idea of Arabia', *American Historical Review*, 111 (2006), pp. 16–52, and 'Developing Iraq: Britain, India, and the Redemption of Empire and Technology in World War I', *Past and Present*, 197 (2007), pp. 211–55; R. M. Douglas, 'Did Britain Use Chemical Weapons in Mandatory Iraq?', *Journal of Modern History*, 81, 4 (2009), pp. 859–87; Aitor Anduaga, *Wireless and Empire: Geopolitics, Radio Industry, and Ionosphere in the British Empire, 1918–1939* (Oxford, 2009); and K. C. Epstein, 'Imperial Airs: Leo Amery, Air Power and Empire, 1873–1945', *Journal of Imperial and Commonwealth History*, 38 (2010), pp. 571–98. On civil aviation, see Peter Lyth, 'The

Empire's Airway: British Civil Aviation from 1919 to 1939', *Revue belge de philologie et d'histoire*, 78 (2000), pp. 865–87.

The last two decades have seen a transformation in our understanding of British armed force. See, for example, David French, *The British Way in Warfare, 1688–2000* (1990), the important special issue of the *International History Review*, 13, 4 (1991), and A. D. Harvey, *Collision of Empires: Britain in Three World Wars, 1793–1945* (1992). My own *Warfare State: Britain 1920–1970* (2005) added to the story, as did George Peden, *Arms, Economics and British Strategy: From Dreadnoughts to Hydrogen Bombs* (Cambridge, 2007), Greg Kennedy (ed.), *Imperial Defence: The Old World Order, 1856–1956* (2007), Keith Neilson and Greg Kennedy (eds.), *The British Way in Warfare: Power and the International System, 1856–1956* (2010) and Joe Maiolo, *Cry Havoc: The Global Arms Race 1931–1941* (2010). In a whole range of other studies, the British case looks very different from what it did – see, for example, Hew Strachan, *Politics of the British Army* (Oxford 1997); David French, *Raising Churchill's Army: The British Army and the War against Germany 1919–1945* (1999), Patrick Wright, *Tank: The Progress of a Monstrous War Machine* (2000), and Jan Rueger, *The Great Naval Game: Britain and Germany in the Age of Empire* (Cambridge, 2007).

Angus Calder, *The Myth of the Blitz* (1991) set a new critical tone for cultural and social histories of the Second World War, also found in David Morgan and Mary Evans, *The Battle for Britain: Citizenship and Ideology in the Second World War* (1993) and Sonya O. Rose, *Which People's War: National Identity and Citizenship in Britain 1939–1945* (Oxford, 2003). My *Britain's War Machine: Weapons, Resources and Experts in the Second World War* (2011) gave a new account from fresh assumptions, developing the one given in this book.

The standard approaches to the histories of the RAF were challenged in J. R. Ferris, 'The Air Force Brats' Views of History: Recent Writing and the Royal Air Force, 1918–1960', *International History Review*, 20 (1995), pp. 118–43. John James, *The Paladins: A*

Social History of the RAF up to the Outbreak of World War 2 (1990) is wonderfully refreshing. Stephen Bungay, *The Most Dangerous Enemy – A History of the Battle of Britain* (2000) showed just how wrong British clichés about the RAF and the Luftwaffe are. Strategic bombing has been the subject of important fresh work, including H. W. Koch, 'The Strategic Air Offensive against Germany: The Early Phase, May–September 1940', *Historical Journal*, 34 (1991), pp. 117–41; Richard Overy, 'The Means to Victory: Bombs and Bombing' in Overy, *Why the Allies Won* (1995), pp. 101–33; Tami Davis Biddle, *Rhetoric and Reality in Air Warfare: The Evolution of British and American Ideas about Strategic Bombing, 1914–1945* (Princeton, 2004); and Paul Addison and Jeremy A. Crang, *Firestorm: The Bombing of Dresden, 1945* (2006). Recruitment to the RAF is discussed in T. Mansell, 'Flying Start: Educational and Social Factors in the Recruitment of Pilots of the Royal Air Force in the Inter-War Years', *History of Education* 26 (1997), pp. 71–90. Randall Thomas Wakelam, *The Science of Bombing: Operational Research in RAF Bomber Command* (Toronto, 2009) shows how science and bombing worked together and not, as in C. P. Snow's fantasies, against each other. I examined the lack of frankness of scientific intellectuals in 'British Scientists and the Relations of Science and War in Twentieth Century Britain', in Paul Forman and J. M. Sanchez Ron (eds.) *National Military Establishments and the Advancement of Science: Studies in Twentieth Century History* (Dordrecht, 1996), pp. 1–35, and in *Warfare State*. Ralph Desmarais disposes of Jacob Bronowski's credibility in these matters in 'Jacob Bronowski: A Humanist Intellectual for an Atomic Age, 1946–1956', *British Journal for the History of Science*, vol. 45 (2012).

Alfred Gollin, *Impact of Air Power* (1990) and Hugh Driver, *The Birth of Military Aviation: Britain, 1903–1914* (1997), added much detail to the pre-1914 story. Edward Packard, 'Whitehall, Industrial Mobilization and the Private Manufacture of Armaments: British

State–Industry Relations, 1918–1936', Ph.D. thesis (London School of Economics, 2009), is particular useful on arms exports. Sebastian Ritchie, *Industry and Air Power: The Expansion of British Aircraft Production, 1935–1941* (1997) is a rich work; see also his 'A New Audit of War: The Productivity of Britain's Wartime Aircraft Industry Reconsidered', *War and Society*, 12 (1994), pp. 125–47. Other insightful work studying the specificities and complexities of aircraft production in relation to the uses of aircraft are Jonathan Zeitlin, 'Flexibility and Mass-Production at War – Aircraft Manufacture in Britain, the United States, and Germany, 1939–1945', *Technology and Culture*, 36 (1995), pp. 46–79, and Erik Lund, 'The Industrial History of Strategy: Reevaluating the Wartime Record of the British Aviation Industry in Comparative Perspective, 1919–1945', *Journal of Military History*, 62 (1998), pp. 75–99. We now have biographies of two key officials in Anthony Furse, *Wilfrid Freeman: The Genius Behind Allied Survival and Air Supremacy, 1939 to 1945* (Staplehurst, 1999) and Terry Jenkins, *Sir Ernest Lemon* (2011). See also Peter Clarke, *The Cripps Version: The Life of Sir Stafford Cripps 1889–1952* (2002), and Alec Cairncross, *Living with the Century* (1999) and his *Planning in Wartime: Aircraft Production in Britain, Germany, and the USA* (1991).

The history of aerodynamics and the technical development of aviation turns out to have been an even richer subject than I imagined. Takehito Hashimoto explored it in 'Theory, Experiment, and Design Practice: The Formation of Aeronautical Research, 1909–1930', Ph.D. thesis (Johns Hopkins University, 1990), and so in effect did Andrew Warwick's *Masters of Theory: Cambridge and the Rise of Mathematical Physics* (2003). Both perspectives were brought together in David Bloor's *Enigma of the Aerofoil: Rival Theories in Aerodynamics, 1909–1930* (Chicago, 2011). Eric Schatzberg, *Wings of Wood, Wings of Metal: Culture and Technical Choice in American Airplane Materials, 1914–1945* (Princeton, 1999) has much to say on the British case too. I developed some critique of idealized models of technical development in my *Shock of the Old: Technology and Global History since 1900* (2006).

The story of the jet engine has advanced apace with Andrew Nahum, 'Two-stroke or Turbine? The Aeronautical Research Committee and British Aeroengine Development in World War II', *Technology and Culture* 38 (1997), pp. 312–54, and his *Frank Whittle: Invention of the Jet* (2nd edn, 2005); Hermione Giffard, 'The Development and Production of Turbojet Aero-engines in Britain, Germany and the United States', Ph.D. thesis (Imperial College London, 2011); and Philip Scranton, 'Mastering Failure: Technological and Organisational Challenges in British and American Military Jet Propulsion, 1943–57', *Business History*, 53 (2011), pp. 479–504. On the wider research and development context, see my *Science, Technology and the British Industrial Decline* (1996), which sets out in detail and with lots of evidence the arguments hinted at in this book. Peter Bowler, *Science for All: The Popularization of Science in Early Twentieth Century Britain* (Chicago, 2009), takes a fresh look at its subject.

Aviation has attracted much attention from cultural historians, for example Michael Paris, *Winged Warfare: The Literature and Theory of Aerial Warfare in Britain, 1859–1917* (Manchester, 1992), *Warrior Nation: Images of War in British Popular Culture, 1850–1992* (2000) and *From the Wright Brothers to 'Top Gun': Aviation, Nationalism and Popular Cinema* (Manchester, 1995). Many other studies are comparative, for example Bernhard Rieger, *Technology and the Culture of Modernity in Britain and Germany, 1890–1945* (Cambridge, 2005); and Robert Wohl, *A Passion for Wings: Aviation and the Western Imagination, 1908–18* (New Haven: 1996) and *The Spectacle of Flight: Aviation and the Western Imagination, 1920–1950* (New Haven, 2005). E. R. Mayhew, *The Reconstruction of Warriors: Archibald McIndoe, the Royal Air Force and the Guinea Pig Club* (2004) and Martin Francis, *The Flyer: British Culture and the Royal Air Force 1939–1945* (Oxford, 2009) both evoke the place of the wartime flyer with subtlety. For Prince Philip's role in promoting aviation and technology more generally, see Richard Weight, *Patriots: National Identity in Britain 1940–2000* (2002), while Simon Winder, *The Man who Saved Britain* (2006) rightly puts the James Bond books firmly into their post-war British context. The landscapes and psycho-geographies of British militarism are now the subject of attention: see Patrick Wright, *The Village that Died for England* (1995 and 2002), and Patrick Keiller's film, *Robinson in Ruins* (2010). I have had the privilege of getting to know Ralph Ehrmann, the man behind the phenomenal success of Airfix kits, a story recounted in Arthur Ward, *Airfix: Celebrating 50 Years of the Greatest Plastic Kits in the World* (1999).

The politics of aviation and aviators has attracted attention. Adrian Smith, *Mick Mannock: Myth, Life and Politics* (2000) is the story of a working-class socialist air ace of the Great War. Noel Pemberton Billing is treated in Philip Hoare, *Oscar Wilde's Last Stand: Decadence, Conspiracy, and the Most Outrageous Trial of the Century* (1999) and is the subject of Barbara Stoney, *Twentieth Century Maverick* (East Grinstead, 2004). On Sempill's spying for Japan until 1941, see Richard Aldrich, *Intelligence and the War Against Japan: Britain, America and the Politics of Secret Service* (Cambridge, 2000). Waqar Zaidi, 'The Janus-face of Techno-nationalism: Barnes Wallis and the "Strength of England"', *Technology and Culture*, 49 (2008), pp. 62–88, spills the beans on the hard-right imperialist and declinist politics of one of Britain's most famous engineers: Barnes Wallis, who ended up a member of the Monday Club, wanted to put 1960s Britain at the centre of the world using swing-wing aircraft and nuclear-powered cargo-carrying submarines. Patrick Zander, '(Right) Wings over Everest: High Adventure, High Technology and High Nationalism on the Roof of the World, 1932–1934' *Twentieth Century British History*, 21 (2011), pp. 300–329, features, among many others, Lady Houston. Michael Weatherburn, in a forthcoming article, has much to say on Sir Arnold Wilson.

British liberal internationalism is now receiving attention more generally: see Peter Wilson and David Long (eds.), *Thinkers of the Twenty Years' Crisis: Inter-War Idealism Reassessed* (Oxford, 1995), my *Warfare State*, and Casper Sylvest, *British Liberal Internationalism, 1880–1930* (Manchester, 2009). Liberal internationalism and the air police has been examined by Waqar Zaidi, '"Aviation Will Either Destroy or Save Our Civilization": Proposals for the Internationalisation of Aviation, 1920–1945', *Journal of Contemporary History*, 46 (2011), pp. 150–78, and '"A Blessing in Disguise": Reconstructing International Relations Through Atomic Energy, 1945–1948', *Past and Present*, 210 (2011; suppl. 6), pp. 309–31. Brett Holman, 'World Police for World Peace: British Internationalism and the Threat of a Knock-out Blow from the Air, 1919–1945', *War in History*, 17 (2010), pp. 313–32, adds to the story as does his magnificent blog, www.airminded.org. See also Andrew Barros, 'Razing Babel and the Problems of Constructing Peace: France, Great Britain, and Air Power, 1916–28', *English Historical Review*, 126 (2011), pp. 75–115. On propaganda in the Second World War, see Gary Campion, *Good Fight: Battle of Britain Propaganda and The Few* (2008). Histories of British wartime film are now numerous, and aeronautical films are prominent in them, but none to my knowledge appreciates the air-brushing of right-wing politics in key aeronautical films of the period. For the post-war years, see Adrian Smith, 'The Dawn of the Jet Age in Austerity Britain: David Lean's *The Sound Barrier* (1952)', *Historical Journal of Film, Radio and Television*, 30 (2010), pp. 487–514.

The technological enthusiasm present in post-war Britain is the subject of Francis Spufford, *Backroom Boys: The Secret Return of the British Boffin* (2003) and James Hamilton-Paterson, *Empire of the Clouds* (2010). I treated post-war policy in much more depth in 'The "White Heat" Revisited: British Government and Technology in the 1960s', *Twentieth Century British History*, 7 (1996), pp. 53–82; and in *Warfare State*.

Jeffrey A. Engel, *Cold War at 30,000 Feet: The Anglo-American Fight for Aviation Supremacy* (Cambridge, Mass., 2007), is a fine study of a central contest. Concorde and international collaboration is well covered in Frances Lynch and Lewis Johnman, 'A Treaty too Far? Britain, France, and Concorde, 1961–1964', *Twentieth Century British History*, 13 (2002), pp. 253–76, and 'The Road to Concorde: Franco-British Relations and the Supersonic Project', *Contemporary European History*, 11, 2 (2002), pp. 229–52; and Frances Lynch, 'Technological Non-Cooperation: Britain and Airbus', *Journal of European Integration History*, 12, 1 (2006), pp. 125–40. On the economics, see Till Geiger, *Britain and the Economic Problem of the Cold War: The Political Economy and the Economic Impact of the British Defence Effort, 1945–1955* (2004). Humphrey Wynn, *RAF Nuclear Deterrent Forces* (1994) covers aeroplanes and rockets. Richard Moore, *Nuclear Illusion, Nuclear Reality: Britain, the United States and Nuclear Weapons, 1958–64* (2010) deals with key issues.

The British rocket programme has got attention, for example Neil Whyte and Philip Gummett, 'Far Beyond the Bounds of Science: The Making of the United Kingdom's First Space Policy', *Minerva*, 35 (1997), pp. 139–69; N. Hill, *A Vertical Empire: The History of the UK Rocket and Space Programme, 1950–1971* (2001); Matthew Godwin, *The Skylark Rocket: British Space Science and the European Space Research Organisation, 1957–1972* (2007); and J. Krige, A. Russo and L Sebasta, *A History of the European Space Agency 1958–1987*, 2 vols (Noordwijk, 2000). See also Wayne Cocroft, '"Dan Dare's Lair": The Industrial Archaeology of Britain's Post-War Technological Renaissance', *Industrial Archaeology Review*, 31 (2009), pp. 5–19. The TSR2 is about the best studied military aircraft: see Sean Straw and John W. Young, 'The Wilson Government and the Demise of TSR-2, October 1964 – April 1965', *Journal of Strategic Studies*, 20, 4 (1997), pp. 18–44, and John Law's *Aircraft Stories: Decentring the Object in Technoscience* (Durham, NC, 2002).

Notes

1. The Strange Birth of Aeronautical England

1 Reginald Pound and Geoffrey Harmsworth, *Northcliffe* (London, 1959), p. 325.
2 *House of Commons Debates*, vol. 8, col. 1566 (2 August 1909).
3 Ibid., col. 1574.
4 Malcolm Cooper, *The Birth of Independent Air Power* (London,1986), p. 3.
5 R. Dallas Brett, *A History of British Aviation, 1908–1914* (London, 1934), p. 128.
6 Geoffrey de Havilland, *Sky Fever* (London, 1961), p. 69.
7 Cooper, *Birth of Independent Air Power*, pp. 4–5.
8 *Royal Commission on the Private Manufacture of and Trading in Arms, 1935/36, Minutes of Evidence* (London, 1935–6), p. 524.
9 *Memorandum on Naval and Military Aviation*, Cd. 6067 (1912), PP1912–13, vol. LI, p. 2.
10 Dallas Brett, *History of British Aviation*, p. 143.
11 David French, *British Economic and Strategic Planning 1905–1915* (London, 1982), p. 23.
12 Umbro Apollonio (ed.), *Futurist Manifestos* (London, 1973), p.22.
13 Jeffrey Meyers, *The Enemy: A Biography of Wyndham Lewis* (London, 1980), p. 62.

14 'Patriotism, Britain and Aerial Efficiency', *Flight*, 26 June 1909.
15 Dallas Brett, *History of British Aviation*, p. 158.
16 Ibid., pp. 48–52.
17 R. H. Fredette, *The Sky on Fire: The First Battle of Britain* (New York, 1966), p. 156.
18 Dallas Brett, *History of British Aviation*, pp. 61–2.
19 Barry D. Powers, *Strategy Without Slide Rule* (London, 1976), pp. 23–4.
20 Alexander de Seversky, the American air power theorist, like Pemberton Billing was a naval aviator, connected with the movies, and the founder of an important aircraft company. Having been a Russian naval aviator in the Great War he made explicit links between naval and air strategy. After the Second World War he called for a 'Pax Democratica' based on American inter-hemispheric air power, by explicit analogy with the naval 'Pax Britannica' of the nineteenth century. His 1941 book *Victory through Air Power* was made into an influential animated film of the same name by Walt Disney in 1943. At Churchill's request it was shown to President Roosevelt at the Quebec Conference the same year. The Seversky Aircraft Corporation, later Republic Aviation, was formed in 1931. Like Supermarine it produced a famous fighter, the Thunderbolt. See Alexander de Seversky, *Air Power: Key to Survival* (London, 1952).
21 Cooper, *Birth of Independent Air Power*, pp. 43–5; Noel Pemberton Billing, *P-B: The Story of his Life* (Hertford: The Imperialist Press, 1917); *Interim Report on the Administration and Command of the Royal Flying Corps, &c* (Chmn: Mr Justice Bailhache) Cd. 8192 (August 1916); *Final Report*, Cd. 8194 (November 1916).

22 In his journal *The Vigilante*, the organ of The Vigilantes, whose object was 'promoting purity in public life', he published an article entitled 'The Cult of the Clitoris'. It implied that a famous avant-garde dancer was a lesbian. She sued, and lost. During the trial, which took place in May and June 1918, Pemberton Billing made the allegation that the Germans had in their possession a Black Book containing the names of 47,000 British 'perverts' in high places, including Herbert Asquith and Lord Haldane, who were being blackmailed to hinder the British war effort. Pemberton Billing resigned from Parliament in 1921 and descended into the murky world of the interwar ultra-right. In 1929 and 1941 he contested by-elections.

23 Fredette, *Sky on Fire*, p. 226.

2. *Technology and Empire*

1 Peter Fearon, 'The British Airframe Industry and the State, 1918–1935', *Economic History Review*, 27 (1974), p. 251.

2 Correlli Barnett, *The Audit of War: The Illusion and Reality of Britain as a Great Nation* (London, 1986), p. 127.

3 Union for Democratic Control, Memorandum, *Royal Commission on the Private Manufacture of and Trading in Arms, 1935/36, Minutes of Evidence* (London, 1935–6), p. 195 [hereafter Royal Commission].

4 Elsbeth E. Freudenthal, 'The Aviation Business in the 1930s', in G. R. Simonson (ed.), *The History of the American Aircraft Industry: An Anthology* (Cambridge, Mass., 1968).

5 Barnett, *Audit of War*, p. 130.

6 Ibid., p. 129.

7 John Ferris, 'Treasury Control: The Ten Year Rule and British Service Policies, 1919–1924', *Historical Journal*, 30 (1987), p. 865.

8 SBAC Memorandum, *Royal Commission*, p. 508.

9 B. Gunston, *By Jupiter! The Life of Sir Roy Fedden* (London, 1978), p. 55.

10 The Union for Democratic Control estimated that the number of RAF squadrons (including Reserve and Auxiliary Air Force Squadrons) equipped by various firms' aircraft in 1934 was: Hawker, 31; Fairey, 17; Handley Page, 1; Armstrong-Whitworth, 1; Vickers, 11; Supermarine, 4; Bristol, 9; Westland, 14; Shorts, 1; Blackburn, 4; Boulton & Paul, 1 (*Royal Commission*, p. 195).

11 *Royal Commission*, p. 434.

12 Noel-Baker Memorandum, *Royal Commission*, p. 280.

13 11 November 1936, p. 588.

14 O. Tapper, *Armstrong Whitworth Aircraft since 1913* (London, 1973).

15 F. K. Mason, *Hawker Aircraft since 1920* (London, 1961), Appendix C.

16 *Royal Commission*, Q. 1078, p. 150.

17 Ibid.

18 Ibid., p. 19, Q. 179; Q. 2498, p. 25.

19 Quoted in W. J. Reader, *Architect of Air Power* (London, 1968), p. 287.

20 *Statement Relating to the Report of the Royal Commission on the Private Manufacture of and Trading in Arms, 1935–1936*, Cmd. 5451.

21 *House of Commons Debates*, vol. 329, col. 431 (1937–8).

22 The problem was to become particularly acute with supersonic aircraft. One commentator suggested the possibility of supersonic flying boats to get round the problem (D. Keith-Lucas, 'The Shape of Wings to Come', *Advancement of Science*, 9 (1952), p. 320).

23 R. MacLeod and A. Andrews, 'The Committee of Civil Research: Scientific Advice for Economic Development, 1925–1930', *Minerva*, 7 (1969), p. 699; D. E. H. Edgerton, 'Science and Technology in British Business History', *Business History*, 29 (1987), pp. 100–102; R. McKinnon Wood, *Aircraft Manufacture* (London: New Fabian Research Bureau, 1935).

24 Malcolm Smith, *British Air Strategy between the Wars* (Oxford, 1984), Table XI, p. 338.

3. Going Up for Air

1 *The Independent*, 14 October 1989.

2 'Cato' [Peter Howard, Michael Foot and Frank Owen], *Guilty Men* (London, 1940), pp. 17–18.

3 Ibid., p. 19.

4 M. J. B. Davy, *Interpretive History of Flight* (London, 1948; first edn, 1937), pp. 130–31.

5 Ibid., p. 139.

6 P. Noel-Baker, 'The International Air Police', in Noel-Baker et al., *Challenge to Death* (London, 1934).

7 Quoted in Volker Berghahn, *Militarism: The History of an International Debate 1861–1979* (Cambridge, 1984), p. 42.

8 Werner Sombart, *The Quintessence of Capitalism* (New York, 1915), p. 331.

9 *Aeronautical Journal*, January 1914, p. 27.

10 Christopher Caudwell, *Studies in a Dying Culture* (London, 1938), pp. 38–9.

11 Ibid., pp. 88–9.

12 Bertrand Russell, *Power* (London, 1975; first edn, 1938), p. 137.

13 Viscount Rothermere, *My Fight to Rearm Britain* (London, 1940), Chapter 9.

14 Quoted in R. Griffiths, *Fellow Travellers of the Right* (London, 1980), p. 25.

15 Ibid., p. 206.

16 Simon Haxey, *Tory MP* (London, 1939), p. 227.

17 Sir Waiter Raleigh, *The War in the Air*, vol. 1 (Oxford, 1922), p. 111.

18 Ibid., p. 121.

19 Ibid., pp. 204–5.

20 *Final Report of the Committee on the Administration and Command of the Royal Flying Corps, &c*, Cd. 8194 (November 1916).

21 C. G. Grey, *British Fighter Planes* (London, 1941), pp. 3–4.

22 Piet Hein Meijering, *Signed with Honour: The Story of Chivalry in Air Warfare* (Edinburgh, 1987), p. 74.

23 J. A. Cross, *Sir Samuel Hoare: A Political Biography* (London, 1977), p. 99.

24 John Terraine, *The Right of the Line* (London, 1988), pp. 462–7.

25 John Pudney, *The Seven Skies* (London, 1959), pp. 120, 131.

4. The Many and the Few

1 Michael Redgrave, *In the Mind's Eye: An Autobiography* (London, 1983), p. 173.
2 Text taken from *Keesing's Contemporary Archives.* The text given in Churchill's collected speeches is slightly different though the sense is identical.
3 *Keesing's Contemporary Archives.*
4 Quoted in J. Terraine, *The Right of the Line* (London, 1988), p. 260.
5 P. M. S. Blackett, *Military and Political Consequences of Atomic Energy* (London, 1948), pp. 16–17.
6 Blackett, *Military and Political Consequences*, p. 28.
7 Terraine, *Right of the Line*, p. 97; Matthew Cooper, *The German Air Force, 1933–1945: An Anatomy of Failure* (London, 1981), p. 93.
8 C. Webster and N. Frankland, *The Strategic Air Offensive Against Germany*, vol. 4 (London, 1961), Appendices 38 and 39.
9 Webster and Frankland, *Strategic Air Offensive*, vol. 4, Appendix 38. Terraine, *Right of the Line*, p. 97, gives slightly different figures for earlier in September 1939.
10 Terraine, *Right of the Line*, p. 682.
11 Roger Eatwell, *The 1945–1951 Labour Government* (London, 1979), p. 44.
12 C. H. Barnes, *Shorts Aircraft since 1900* (London, 1967), pp. 30–31.
13 Joseph Schumpeter, *Capitalism, Socialism and Democracy* (London, 1976), p. 375.

14 Quoted in R. P. Shay, *British Rearmament in the Thirties: Politics and Profits* (Princeton, 1977), p. 94.
15 Quoted in B. Gunston, *By Jupiter! The Life of Sir Roy Fedden* (London, 1978), p. 91.
16 Malcolm Smith, *British Air Strategy Between the Wars* (Oxford, 1984), p. 47.
17 M. M. Postan, D. Hay and J. D. Scott, *Design and Development of Weapons* (London, 1964), p. 15.
18 SBAC Memorandum for the Secretary of State for Air's Industrial Advisory Panel, 21 June 1938. PRO AVIA 10/20.
19 C. Bruce Gardner (SBAC) to Colonel Llewellin (Minister of Aircraft Production), 15 May 1942, HP AC 70/10/57. Handley Page Archives, Royal Air Force Museum, Hendon.
20 Ministry of Aircraft Production, *The Aircraft Builders* (London, 1947), p. 80.
21 Barnes, *Shorts Aircraft*, p. 31.
22 *Picture Post*, 17 April 1943, quoted in R. Croucher, *The Engineers at War, 1939–1945* (London, 1982), p. 202.
23 W. W. Astor, *House of Commons Debates*, vol. 399, col. 158 (31 March 1943).
24 Correlli Barnett, *The Audit of War* (London, 1986), p. 146.
25 To calculate British productivity for 1944 as a whole, and for March 1944 he uses the same figure for employment, 510,000, which seems to be a figure for 1943 (ibid., p. 146). He gives Public Record Office reference CAB 87/13 PR(43)98 as his source. The (43) in this reference dates the document 1943! More importantly, he converts yearly and monthly output figures per worker into output per day

figures by dividing by 365 and 31, respectively. For example 1944: 221,985,000 lb ÷ 365 ÷ 510,000 = 1.19 lb per man day (p. 321, note 23); March 1944: 20,300,000 lb ÷ 31 ÷ 510,000 = 1.28 (p. 323, note 106). But even if every day of the year was a working day, it was not the case that all the workers employed were working every day of the year. Thus if the German figures were calculated on the same basis it may simply be that Germans had a higher 'productivity' because they worked longer hours.

26 Eric Mensforth, 'Airframe Production', *Proceedings of the Institution of Mechanical Engineers*, 156 (1947), pp. 24–38.
27 E. Devons, *Planning in Practice: Essays in Aircraft Planning in Wartime* (Cambridge, 1950), p. 150. He noted that there lingered in MAP 'the impression that it was possible in some way to measure the efficiency of the production process quite separately from the usefulness of what was produced' (p. 150).
28 Richard Overy, *Goering: The 'Iron Man'* (London, 1984), pp. 148–85.
29 Ibid., p. 177.
30 He notes that by 1939 parity with Germany was achieved, but suggests this was due to the continued production of obsolete types (Barnett, *Audit of War*, p. 142). This is certainly true, but the implication that all German aircraft were first class is not established.
31 Ibid., p. 156.
32 R. J. Overy, *The Air War 1939–1945* (London, 1980), p. 174.
33 Ibid., p. 174.
34 Barnett, *Audit of War*, p. 156.

5. The Sonic Boom of the Scientific Revolution

1 Anthony Barnett, *Iron Britannia* (London, 1982), and *New Left Review*, 134 (1982).
2 James Hinton, *Protests and Visions* (London, 1988).
3 Gavin de Beer, *The Sciences Were Never at War* (Cambridge, 1961); C. P. Snow, 'The Moral Un-Neutrality of Science' (1960), reprinted in *The Physicists* (London, 1988); Jacob Bronowski, *The Common Sense of Science* (London, 1951), Chapter 9.
4 Robert Jungk, *Brighter Than a Thousand Suns* (London, 1958).
5 'Scientific revolution' because Harold Wilson used the phrase rather than 'technological revolution': '... in all our plans for the future, we are re-defining and we are restating our Socialism in terms of the scientific revolution. But that revolution cannot become a reality unless we are prepared to make far-reaching changes in economic and social attitudes which permeate our whole system of society. The Britain that is going to be forged in the white heat of this revolution will be no place for restrictive practices or for outdated methods on either side of industry.' (Speech opening the Science Debate at the Party's Annual Conference, Scarborough, 1963, in Harold Wilson, *Purpose in Politics: Selected Speeches* (London, 1964), p. 27).
6 Quoted in D. E. H. Edgerton, 'Technical Innovation, Industrial Capacity and Efficiency: Public Ownership and the British Military Aircraft Industry, 1935–1948', *Business History*, 26 (1984), pp. 269–70.

7 Quoted in Sir Frank Whittle, *Jet: The Story of a Pioneer* (London, 1953), p. 263.

8 Ibid., p. 302.

9 Quoted in R. Miliband, *Parliamentary Socialism*, 2nd edn (London, 1972), p. 300.

10 Michael Dockrill, *British Defence Since 1945* (London, 1988), Appendix IV.

11 *Daily Express*, 13 August 1968.

12 Tony Benn, *Against the Tide: Diaries, 1973–1976* (London, 1989), p. 214.

13 Charles Gardner, *British Aircraft Corporation: A History* (London, 1981), p. 275.

14 'Innovation, Investment and the Survival of the UK Economy' (speech at the Institution of Mechanical Engineers, 14 July 1989).

15 Andrew Gamble, *Britain in Decline* (London, 1981), p. 180.

16 Aubrey Jones, *Britain's Economy: The Roots of Stagnation* (Cambridge, 1985), pp. 81–5; Appendix 1.

6. Conclusion

1 'With Stopwatch in Hand', in Harry Zohn (ed.), *In These Great Times: A Karl Kraus Reader* (Manchester, 1984), p. 141.

2 George Orwell, 'As I Please', *Tribune*, 12 May 1944, in *The Collected Essays, Journalism and Letters of George Orwell*, vol. 3, *As I Please* (Harmondsworth, 1970), p. 173.

3 George Orwell, 'You and the Atom Bomb', *Collected Essays*, vol. 4, p. 25.

4 Thomas Pynchon, *Gravity's Rainbow* (London, 1975), p. 520.

Index

ALLEN LANE
an imprint of
PENGUIN BOOKS

Recently Published

David Graeber, *The Democracy Project: A History, a Crisis, a Movement*

Brendan Simms, *Europe: The Struggle for Supremacy, 1453 to the Present*

Oliver Bullough, *The Last Man in Russia and the Struggle to Save a Dying Nation*

Diarmaid MacCulloch, *Silence: A Christian History*

Evgeny Morozov, *To Save Everything, Click Here: Technology, Solutionism, and the Urge to Fix Problems that Don't Exist*

David Cannadine, *The Undivided Past: History Beyond Our Differences*

Michael Axworthy, *Revolutionary Iran: A History of the Islamic Republic*

Jaron Lanier, *Who Owns the Future?*

John Gray, *The Silence of Animals: On Progress and Other Modern Myths*

Paul Kildea, *Benjamin Britten: A Life in the Twentieth Century*

Jared Diamond, *The World Until Yesterday: What Can We Learn from Traditional Societies?*

Nassim Nicholas Taleb, *Antifragile: How to Live in a World We Don't Understand*

Alan Ryan, *On Politics: A History of Political Thought from Herodotus to the Present*

Roberto Calasso, *La Folie Baudelaire*

Carolyn Abbate and Roger Parker, *A History of Opera: The Last Four Hundred Years*

Yang Jisheng, *Tombstone: The Untold Story of Mao's Great Famine*

Caleb Scharf, *Gravity's Engines: The Other Side of Black Holes*

Jancis Robinson, Julia Harding and José Vouillamoz, *Wine Grapes: A Complete Guide to 1,368 Vine Varieties, including their Origins and Flavours*

David Bownes, Oliver Green and Sam Mullins, *Underground: How the Tube Shaped London*

Niall Ferguson, *The Great Degeneration: How Institutions Decay and Economies Die*

Chrystia Freeland, *Plutocrats: The Rise of the New Global Super-Rich*

David Thomson, *The Big Screen: The Story of the Movies and What They Did to Us*

Halik Kochanski, *The Eagle Unbowed: Poland and the Poles in the Second World War*

Kofi Annan with Nader Mousavizadeh, *Interventions: A Life in War and Peace*

Mark Mazower, *Governing the World: The History of an Idea*

Anne Applebaum, *Iron Curtain: The Crushing of Eastern Europe 1944-56*

Steven Johnson, *Future Perfect: The Case for Progress in a Networked Age*

Christopher Clark, *The Sleepwalkers: How Europe Went to War in 1914*

Neil MacGregor, *Shakespeare's Restless World*

Nate Silver, *The Signal and the Noise: The Art and Science of Prediction*

Chinua Achebe, *There Was a Country: A Personal History of Biafra*

John Darwin, *Unfinished Empire: The Global Expansion of Britain*

Jerry Brotton, *A History of the World in Twelve Maps*

Patrick Hennessey, *KANDAK: Fighting with Afghans*

Katherine Angel, *Unmastered: A Book on Desire, Most Difficult to Tell*

David Priestland, *Merchant, Soldier, Sage: A New History of Power*

Stephen Alford, *The Watchers: A Secret History of the Reign of Elizabeth I*

Tom Feiling, *Short Walks from Bogotá: Journeys in the New Colombia*

Pankaj Mishra, *From the Ruins of Empire: The Revolt Against the West and the Remaking of Asia*

Geza Vermes, *Christian Beginnings: From Nazareth to Nicaea, AD 30-325*

Steve Coll, *Private Empire: ExxonMobil and American Power*

Joseph Stiglitz, *The Price of Inequality*

Dambisa Moyo, *Winner Take All: China's Race for Resources and What it Means for Us*

Robert Skidelsky and Edward Skidelsky, *How Much is Enough? The Love of Money, and the Case for the Good Life*

Frances Ashcroft, *The Spark of Life: Electricity in the Human Body*

Sebastian Seung, *Connectome: How the Brain's Wiring Makes Us Who We Are*

Callum Roberts, *Ocean of Life*

Orlando Figes, *Just Send Me Word: A True Story of Love and Survival in the Gulag*

Leonard Mlodinow, *Subliminal: The Revolution of the New Unconscious and What it Teaches Us about Ourselves*

John Romer, *A History of Ancient Egypt: From the First Farmers to the Great Pyramid*

Ruchir Sharma, *Breakout Nations: In Pursuit of the Next Economic Miracle*

Michael J. Sandel, *What Money Can't Buy: The Moral Limits of Markets*

Dominic Sandbrook, *Seasons in the Sun: The Battle for Britain, 1974-1979*

Tariq Ramadan, *The Arab Awakening: Islam and the New Middle East*

Jonathan Haidt, *The Righteous Mind: Why Good People are Divided by Politics and Religion*

Ahmed Rashid, *Pakistan on the Brink: The Future of Pakistan, Afghanistan and the West*

Tim Weiner, *Enemies: A History of the FBI*

Mark Pagel, *Wired for Culture: The Natural History of Human Cooperation*